BANTAISM II

Bhai Niranjan Singh 'Amrikawale' grew up in Delhi and lives in the USA. His articles on politics and current affairs have appeared in print and online publications in India and America. In other lives, he has worked for a bank and run two software companies.

This is his second book on the philosophy of sardar jokes.

BANTAISM
II

THE METAPHYSICS OF
MAINNU KI

BHAI NIRANJAN SINGH
'AMRIKAWALE'

Illustrated by
Priyankar Gupta

RUPA

Published by
Rupa Publications India Pvt. Ltd 2015
7/16, Ansari Road, Daryaganj
New Delhi 110002

Sales centres:

Allahabad Bengaluru Chennai
Hyderabad Jaipur Kathmandu
Kolkata Mumbai

Copyright © Niranjan Ramakrishnan 2015

The views and opinions expressed in this book are the author's own and the publishers are not in any way liable for the same. Names, characters, places and incidents are either the product of the author's imagination or are used fictitiously and any resemblance to any actual person, living or dead, events or locales is entirely coincidental.

All rights reserved.
No part of this publication may be reproduced, transmitted, or stored in a retrieval system, in any form or by any means, electronic, mechanical, photocopying, recording or otherwise, without the prior permission of the publisher.

ISBN: 978-81-291-3585-8

First impression 2015

10 9 8 7 6 5 4 3 2 1

The moral right of the author has been asserted.

Printed at Thomson Press India Ltd, Faridabad

This book is sold subject to the condition that it shall not, by way of trade or otherwise, be lent, resold, hired out, or otherwise circulated, without the publisher's prior consent, in any form of binding or cover other than that in which it is published.

To the memory of Lalitha Periamma for her boundless affection, generosity of heart and all the wonderful holidays in Feroze Shah Road

Common sense and a sense of humor are the same thing, moving at different speeds. A sense of humor is just common sense, dancing.

—William James

A Note on the Notables

A few eminent public figures appear in these jokes. The stories in this book, including those involving them, are apocryphal, in no way to be confused with real-life personas.

Preface

When *Bantaism* was published back in November 2011, it was my first book. In due deference, I ordered copies and sent them to all the elders in the family. I told friends about the book. As loved ones are wont, all sent their blessings and good wishes. Some of them may even have read it; many did send me ten or twenty copies as presents. Several told me they found it an ideal gift for their friends.

This was all to the good. But there comes a time when an author wonders whether anyone outside the family and friends' circle has even heard of his work. So it was that a few months down I mustered the courage to seek official word.

'Sir, the book is doing well in airports,' answered the lady from the publisher's sales office. Over time, corroboration trickled in. Friends recalled how they had seen it featured on the shelves of various airport bookstores. This brought back to mind how an old classmate had responded to my note telling him about the book—he had emailed right back saying that he was already aware of the book, having purchased a copy at the airport on his way back to the US. And to cap it all was another email, received two years after the book's publication, written in a tone of breathless excitement entirely incongruous with the austere reserve one expects of jet-setting international civil servants of high rank, 'I am at Delhi airport, waiting for my flight back to the US. As usual, I made my obligatory stop at the bookstore (WH Smith). Again, as usual, I looked for *Bantaism* and was delighted to see that it is still in the shelf of bestsellers!'

Why the book should attract air travellers is a mystery to which I will not pretend to have an answer. Perhaps because the reader can peruse the volume amidst strangers and leave it behind on the plane, thereby hiding his indiscretion from the near and dear ones? A last-minute attempt to assuage the spouse back home at the end of a long business trip? '*Oye, ki m'loom* (Hey, who knows)?' is Banta's own guideline on such matters. Under the circumstances, it might even be a fit case for that brahmaastra[1], '*Oye, Mainnu ki* (What's it to me)?' After all, it isn't every author who can claim, and with a straight face, that his book appeared to be literally 'flying off the shelves'!

Bantaism found mention in the newspapers as well. The book received favourable notice in *The Tribune* and *Kannada Prabha*. A number of bloggers commented on it, all of whom thought its approach novel, and several even wrote some nice things about it. The publishing house and I had independently sent a copy to (the now late) Sardar Khushwant Singh, who wrote about it in his very next

---

[1]The supreme weapon

column. He lauded its audacity, but disparaged the notion of there being any philosophical merit in the book. In a short note sent along with the first copy of *Bantaism*, I had addressed Mr Singh as the 'doyen of sardar jokes'. That he was also an expert in philosophy was a revelation. The other three-quarters of his review consisted of a verbatim reproduction of jokes and commentary from the book!

At some point during all this, the publisher, too, got taken in. Not only did he authorize a second edition of the book, but went to the extent of suggesting a sequel. Now, the sequel is ever a slippery affair. How many times has it not proved the nemesis of names, the robber of reputations, the exploder of eminences! Perfectly suited, he no doubt reasoned, to an author unencumbered by any such baggage. The thought had also vaguely occurred to me from time to time, ever since a friend had cried discrimination when told about *Bantaism*. 'Why no "Santaism"?' he protested, in a manner reminiscent of Banta Singh when he came to know of the airport[2] in Bombay ('Oye, what about thee Banta Cruz oye?').

Besides, there is the customer's welfare to think about. In the times we live in, consumer choice is the phrase on everyone's lips. And speaking of choices and other slippery affairs that dominate our lives:

Infra Digg[3]

Each morning at precisely the same time, Banta Singh

---

[2]Santa Cruz Airport
[3]'Digg' is Punjabi for 'fall down'

walks from his home to the office, and along precisely the same route. As it happens, there lives on the second story of a building overlooking Banta's path an equally punctilious old gentleman. Every day, like clockwork, he finishes his breakfast consisting of coffee, a slice of toast and a banana. When he is done, he tosses the banana peel onto the pavement below, exactly a couple of minutes before Banta turns the corner and reaches the spot. And each morning, without fail, Banta steps on the fresh peel, takes a toss, then gets up, dusts himself off, and proceeds onward to his office. One day, the man on the second floor decides to have some extra nourishment, and ends up tossing two banana peels instead of one on to the sidewalk. Banta turns the corner shortly thereafter, and comes to a sudden halt. A look of delight appears on his face. He exclaims, '*Oye, ajj tah choass haigi hai* (Wow, today there's choice)!'

And there is a maximalist choice too. In another variation of the punchline, Banta laments upon seeing the two peels, '*Hai rabba, ajj do vaari diggna paina hai* (Oh God, I have to fall twice today)!'

I wonder, too, if this business of *Bantaism* finding favour at the airport is not in itself some kind of a subliminal indication for a sequel. In the first book, I had noted the long and hoary connection between the railways and the sardar jokes. An association forged in steel and laughter, it is as unbreakable as they come (just see the first joke in this book). Nonetheless, the sardar joke too must keep up with the times; as you will see—the fax machine, the photocopier, the cellphone, not forgetting, the computer and the printer—all figure in this volume.

As with *Bantaism*, none of the jokes in this book are my creation; only their selection, headings, retelling and comments. My sole claim to anything approaching an 'original' contribution in this department is an ostensible crossword clue, 'Rift in Akali ranks sounds like a matter of faith (6 letters)'.[4]

And as with *Bantaism* (see Author's Note reproduced in this volume), it is best to read this book in small doses, no more than perhaps a joke or two a day.

Aeniway, however you read it, just anjway!

Niranjan Ramakrishnan
USA, January 2014

---

[4]Schism

Author's Note

I couldn't have been more than seven or eight when I heard my first sardar[1] joke. It opened for me, as someone said of P.G. Wodehouse's novels, 'a world to live and delight in'. I have treasured ever since each gem that has come my way.

But it was only in college, several years later, that I first ran across Banta Singh. He figured in some jokes told by a Punjabi classmate, an outstanding raconteur. Incidentally, Banta's associate those days was Bachittar Singh not Santa, just as his wife bore the stately name of Kulwant Kaur instead of the Preeto or Jeeto she has since become. In time, this new character, like Mulla Nasruddin or Father Brown, would come to acquire a universal persona of his own.

The invention of Banta Singh seems to have achieved two purposes. For the joke-teller, the very name is a godsend. It trips off the tongue. It is delightfully rustic, rotund, funny, broadly benign with a whiff of low craft—a

---

[1] Sardar is a term used for 'leader' or 'head' or 'chief' in many parts of Asia, including Afghanistan, Pakistan and India. In India, it is mainly used for adult male members in Sikh families

concoction guaranteed to provoke a laugh just by its mention. Its other task, perhaps not originally envisaged, is as a fig-leaf in our increasingly touchy times—to provide a pretense that this is not really about sardars; it is just about one lone guy called Banta Singh. I've always thought this was a pathetic cop-out, even disingenuous. Banta Singh without the 'sardar' identity is like Hamlet without the Prince of Denmark. Banta is to sardardom what Homer Simpson is to America, a caricature entirely imperfect but wholly irresistible; Homer is certainly not American, but you cannot conceive of his being from anywhere else.

Meanwhile that traditional staple, *ik vaari ik sardar si...* (once there was a sardar...)—the Classic Coke of the sardar joke—continues to march along, as everyone knows it will: some jokes are just naturally *ik-vaari-ik-sardar-si*'s. And Banta Singh too is here to stay; with a name like his it could not be otherwise. Both have their own place, and that's all there is to it. How does one decide when to use which? For a hint of how to resolve such conundrums we have only to look to the master himself.

'Oye Banteya, how do you tell whether a chick is a murga (rooster) or murgi (hen)?' someone once asked Banta Singh.

'*Koi vaddi gal ni* (It's no big deal). I feed it some rice and then observe carefully,' replied Banta, '*je khaooga ta murga hai, je khaoogi ta murgi hai* (if *he* eats it, it's a rooster, if *she* eats it, it's a hen).'

From whom to feature in a sardar joke, we move to a more fraught question: whether to tell a sardar joke. With all due respect to the political correctness police, I think it is an insult to the average citizen to say he needs to be shielded from certain kinds of jokes on the chance that he may believe something he hears as the gospel truth (an especially lame plea in an era when even the gospel has trouble passing as the gospel truth). The simplest of folk have sophistication enough to separate the real nature of individuals/communities from the apocrypha about them. For me this was brought home—not literally, for all my jokes came from friends and classmates and other adults outside—early. I noticed even as a youngster that, while all kinds of people regaled one another with sardar jokes, Sikhs were in general well regarded. They were seldom addressed other than as 'sardarji', and treated with a respect sometimes bordering on deference and awe, stemming perhaps in part from some feeling of guilt.

Of their reputation for physical bravery, courage and sacrifice, no Indian needs to be told; a cursory acquaintance with history would do. But growing up in New Delhi with its large Sikh population, I came to learn that they also tended to be among India's most hard-working, open and large-hearted citizens, albeit quick to anger.

The urban Sikh was not unoften the most urbane of Indians. It was even reputed that many sardar jokes were made up by sardars themselves. Impossible to verify, of course, but if true, there can be no greater tribute to the sardar intelligence. Or self-confidence. I do know that the use of expressions like, '*Oye, tu aadmi hai ki sardar?* (Are you human or sardar?)', or '*sardaraan waali gal* (sardar logic)' was common in gently debunking any perceived infirmities of reason. That such things could be said as freely to a Sikh, even inviting a smiling repartee on occasion, 'Oye, jaddon hain hi sardar ta sardaraan waali gal kivain ni karaange (When one is a sardar, how can one avoid sardarspeak)?' said volumes about the self-esteem and sense of humour of the Sikhs. Indians are usually happiest making fun of everyone else while wearing the thinnest of skins themselves. Sikhs seemed to be a wonderful exception to this norm.

Into this happy world, some unknown public school lads of the 1960s introduced another term: surd. My guess is that it came out of S.L. Loney's classic text on mathematics. The word originally meant irrational number. Given the nature of the sardar joke, it is easy to imagine that this fact must have struck its purveyors as a serendipity exceeding their wildest dreams. Whatever its etymology, 'surd' soon gained currency in city school and college campuses, at least the English-breathing ones. The chai shop near the IIT Delhi campus, for instance, was known as 'surd shop' because it was run by a sardar. No one gave it a second thought (no pun intended).

All this easy back and forth started to change in the early 1980s. The Indian government got involved in a dangerous game, playing with fire for nothing more than a transient political advantage. They tried to offset their mainstream political opponents in Punjab by encouraging the most obscurantist (and mostly humourless) fringes within the Sikh community. What followed was a decade-

and-a-half of pure tragedy, human and political, an effort by enemies of India 'to alienate Sikhs from Hindus, and to alienate them from the Indian state' (quoting roughly from what an Indian journalist wrote at that time). This is not the place to get into the march of crime and folly by the Indian government, the murderous violence by the Sikh terrorists, the harassment of Sikhs during the 1982 Asiad, the army raid on the Golden Temple, Prime Minister Indira Gandhi's killing, the anti-Sikh pogrom that followed and the abuses perpetrated by all sides on Punjab for the next decade.

From the viewpoint of sardar jokes, this traumatic time saw a progressive thinning of the Sikh skin, a rise in intolerance, the surfacing of an uncharacteristic atavism and the appearance of one sure sign of a diminished self-esteem—a perpetual ear cocked for slights real and imagined. For good measure, many of these developments received encouragement from some Sikhs abroad. It is paradoxical that the progressiveness of a community in India appears these days to be in inverse proportion to how many of its numbers are settled in the West!

I received something by way of an explanation many years ago from a niece of Sardar Swaran Singh, former defense and external affairs minister of India. I ran into her not in India but in Vancouver, BC, where she lived. Her father (Swaran Singh's elder brother) had settled there in 1903! She said that emigrants like her tended to 'hold on' to an India that may no longer exist.

All said and done, I feel that the Sikh in India is far

less insecure than his cohorts in the UK, USA or Canada. Yet, the Indian Sikh was the primary victim of many crimes leading to death, dismemberment or disruption in Punjab, instigated and carried out at the behest of some among these same immigrant communities in the name of 'honour' or 'dignity'. There is little more heinous than fostering mayhem from a safe distance, worse, for nothing more than perceived injury to pride. Often these are also the same folk who express elaborate hurt at some imagined slight in the lands of their domicile. Long years of exposure to the putative openness and tolerance of the West appears to have had little impact. A few years ago, a play scheduled to open in the UK had to be cancelled and the playwright and actors reportedly went into hiding, because of death threats from some Sikh groups who found the drama's theme objectionable. The British government, whose duty one presumes is to protect the lives, liberties and freedom of expression of its citizens, appeared to be helpless, or simply not to care.

The way I see it, every part of the world has its own favourite ethnic/professional/sectional joke. In Delhi, where I grew up, it was the sardar joke. Later, as I was exposed to humour from other regions of the globe, it was clear that jokes travelled, with the character modified to suit the locale. Figuratively then, Mulla Nasruddin might discard the thobe and get into a pair of slacks to figure in the Polish joke, then don a turban and beard for his forthcoming trip to Delhi or Amritsar. The genius of the joke lay as much in the cleverness of adaptation as in its essence.

Why this book? I have spent the major portion of my career in the software world. In the course of my work, I was surprised to find that a number of illustrative examples pertaining to conceptual, design and business issues could be drawn directly from sardar jokes. Later I discovered the same thing with some of my writings on politics and current affairs (as the saying goes, to a man with a hammer everything begins to look like a nail—maybe I'd heard too many sardar jokes).

Still, one is frequently dumbstruck at finding some patently implausible chutkula[2] being enacted almost verbatim, not by Banta and Bachittar but by supposedly wise world-statesmen. It slowly dawned on me that the sardar joke was a lot bigger than the garden-variety gag. Instead, it was showing itself to be deep, philosophical, profound and universal!

If the American baseball star Yogi Berra can be called a philosopher and have his sayings celebrated as Yogi-isms, is there any reason why our own Banta Singh's glories cannot spawn their unique brand of wisdom? To reach for that most elemental of tenets from the Punjabi weltanschauung, *Assi kede maade haan* (Why, what's wrong with us)?' Thus Bantaism.

Kipling wrote, 'What do they know of England who only England know.' So it is with those who think the sardar joke is about the sardar. In my own case, I've found myself identifying with practically every variety of folly

---

[2]Joke

in every sardar joke. I seem to have replicated many, if not most of them. Often the jokes are but send-ups of a mind fixed in its ways and resistant to any but its own accustomed modes of operation. Nor can I boast of being so far outside the mainstream as to claim any exclusive ownership of such debacles. I feel certain that we have all had our share of set ways, blinkered reasoning and associated lunacies. Through the rustic foibles of Banta and his friends, we are gently reminded that the joke really is on us and all our pretensions. To paraphrase the headline in a French newspaper the morning after 9/11: WE ARE ALL SARDARS NOW.[3] Or if you prefer, *'Hun assaan saare Bante haan* (We are all Banta Singhs now).'

Another thing to keep in mind. Several jokes that did not appear to me very deep at the outset, took on a definite philosophical hue over time—sometimes with a startling suddenness. That is, I had to grow mature enough to 'get it'. This process may itself be best illustrated by—what else?—a sardar joke heard long ago, told by a sardarni[4] at a social gathering, to the laughter of her heart-patient father, her mother, and her husband, all Sikhs:

> When the Alfred Hitchcock thriller, *Psycho*, came to town, everyone was eager to see it, including the sardarji. His family was totally opposed to the idea, though, because he had a serious heart condition and had been advised against undue excitement or shock. But he was

---

[3] 'We Are All Americans Now', *Le Monde*, 12 September 2001
[4] Sikh lady

insistent, and in the end they were forced to take him along when they went to see the film.

To everyone's surprise, he did just fine after seeing *Psycho*. Then one fine day, three months later, he died suddenly of a heart attack.

Word on the street was that the sardar had died as soon as he understood the movie (*jaddon picture samajh aayi taan ose vele mar gaya*).

My aim with this book is threefold: to capture the best sardar jokes, to examine their deeper meaning and to make their narration easy.

How should you read a book like this? My only advice is, go slow. Imagine the characters, visualize the situation and roll the words over. And remember, no more than one or two jokes a day. Give it time. Let it settle. Like enjoying fine wine, to '*vail thee full ban-fit*'[5], the sardar joke too must be savoured on many levels. The true connoisseur will let a picture settle in his imagination, let the words sprinkle over it, then allow the whole scenario to run through his head a few times, until without his knowing a smile spreads slowly across his face. There is no feeling equal to it.

Should you decide to tell sardar jokes, it is best to get some practice first. To get you started, the jokes in this book are written as they might be read out to an audience.

You'll get a little more out of the book and a lot more out of your renditions if you can read the Punjabi (you

---

[5]Translation: avail of the full benefit

don't have to know the language) out loud. I've tried to supply the words and the translation, but reading out the English in a suitable cadence is often perfectly adequate.

Translating the Punjabi gaali[6] is a different matter, however, for it is its own wonderland. Here you will have to manage without my help. Wherever you see something like ^&%$^, use your imagination—freely, but knowing you may yet fall short.

A final note: the book contains some of my favourite sardar jokes, but not one of these is my own. I have merely gathered them, lovingly over the years, from friends and colleagues, and in more recent times from email forwards. My only claim to originality lies in the titles, the retelling and observations which, where I have any, are provided immediately following the joke. As you read, I'm sure you will have your own epiphanies (well, epi-funnies, at any rate).

Enjoy (oye, just anjway)!

Niranjan Ramakrishnan
New Delhi, May 2010

---

[6]Punjabi, the language spoken by most Sikhs, is famous for its rich and colourful swear words and oaths, known as gaalis. Technically, gaali is a Hindi word, the Punjabi word for it is gaal. Cultural sociolinguists may make what they will out of the fact that it differs by a single letter from the word gal (pronounced as in seagull), which is the Punjabi word for 'talk' or 'matter'

Cross-platform Compatibility

Late one summer evening, the local news station received word of a huge accident at the Faridkot railway station. They rushed a young reporter and photo crew immediately to the scene.

What the reporter found was horrific. It appeared that a large party of sardars had been hit by the Punjab Mail as it was pulling in. Inside the station was a total pandemonium—ambulance sirens wailing in the background, emergency personnel trying to save the injured, relatives searching for their loved ones, officials yelling orders to their subordinates, police trying to keep the peace, curious onlookers milling about and getting in the way. No one seemed to know what the victims were doing on the railway track. Asking around, all that the reporter was able to ascertain was this: the group appeared to have been waiting, quite normally, for the train to pull in so that they could board it. Suddenly there had been a big panic and the entire lot had jumped off the railway platform and on to the tracks, en masse. Why they should have done so was a mystery no one seemed to be able to explain.

It was at this point that the reporter suddenly noticed

a middle-aged sardar standing in the far corner, away from all the commotion. What particularly caught her eye was his expression; somehow it seemed to her that he might be connected with the group. Deciding to check out her hunch, she made her way through the crowds towards the man.

She found him in a state of complete shock. By and by she managed to get him to talk. His name, he said, was Banta Singh.

Yes, indeed, he was with this very group. They had come, as the reporter had learned before, to catch the train to Delhi. 'What had happened?' she asked softly.

'They were scared by the announcement,' Banta answered. 'We were all waiting for the train when it was announced over the PA system that the Delhi bound train was coming on platform number 1. Naturally since they were on the platform, they wanted to avoid it, and there was nowhere to go but the tracks,' his voice trailed off. The reporter was still trying to digest this when another thought occurred to her. 'They thought it was coming right on the platform? Good God! But thank goodness, you knew that's not what the announcement meant!'

'No, madam. Actually, I was already standing on the tracks. You see...I was with them...but I had really come here to commit suicide. When I heard the announcement of the train coming on the platform, I jumped from the tracks on to the platform so it didn't miss me.'

Commentary

Much has been written about the madness of crowds. Just from recent memory, the stock market bubble, the housing bubble, stampedes in various places owing to rumours of a bridge collapse or a building fire, all tell us that this is not uncommon. The beauty of the joke is how well it shows a perfectly reasoned approach could be as much based on a uniform misunderstanding.

It is also a commentary on the public address system, often a purveyor of garbled cacophony which makes even the most benign communication sound like an intimation of impending disaster. Nothing raises the blood pressure like a loudspeaker announcement at the airport or at the train station.

Finally, it is a telling example of the importance of precision in language, particularly in the use of the preposition. As Bhabani Bhattacharya observes in his book, *Gandhi, the Writer*, 'Edward Thompson gives us a pleasing account of Gandhi's mastery over English. "The hardest thing in our language for a foreigner," he says, "is our prepositions. I never met an Indian who had mastered them as Gandhi has."'[1]

In Punjabi, as also in many other Indian languages, 'at' does not, to my knowledge, have an exact equivalent. In Hindi, 'par' and 'pe' (both meaning, 'on') as well as 'ko' (meaning, 'to') are used to convey the sense of the

---

[1] *Gandhi, the Writer: the Image as It Grew* by Bhabani Bhattacharya, National Book Trust, 1969, p. 111

English word, 'at'. In Punjabi, 'vich', strictly speaking 'in the middle of' or 'amidst' or 'in', is used to do the same. Thus, the Punjabi announcement for 'Punjab Mail going to New Delhi is arriving at platform number one' might be: *'Ni Dilli jaan vaali Punjab Mail hunn platform number ik vich aa ree hai.'*

Vich vaas probably what caused all the trouble!

Regressingh

Santa Singh was in the Army. His young son was just getting to be of school-going age when Santa received orders posting him to a remote location. He decided to take his family along, intending to home-school the boy during his three-year stint; there were no suitable schools where he was being posted. And so he did, earnestly, teaching the youngster for three years as best he could.

When he was posted back to a large town, three years later, Santa took his son down to the finest school in the vicinity. He told the school authorities of how he had educated the child himself, sparing no effort, and succeeded in persuading them to admit the boy directly into the third grade.

Some weeks went by. Then one day the school principal called up requesting Santa to come over for a meeting. The teachers had found the boy not ready for the third grade, and wanted him moved to the second instead. Santa was not happy, but he agreed. Schooling had certainly moved along since his day, he reasoned. Perhaps what he, Santa, had learned in third grade was now being taught in the second.

From the next day on, the son began going to the second grade. A few weeks later, the principal invited Santa to the school once more. 'I'm sorry to have to tell you this, Mr Singh, but I'm afraid your son isn't quite ready for the second grade. We all feel he needs to be demoted to first grade. It is really in his interest...' They showed him what other students of the grade were doing, and the boy's own progress.

Santa headed home straight from the school, his face sombre. '*Oye biwi*,' he whispered to his wife when she opened the door, his voice laden with foreboding, '*hunn apna pajama kass lai, ke munda sadda revarse gear'ch aa riha hai* (Hey wife, you better hold on tight to your pajamas, this lad of ours might be coming in the reverse gear)'.

Commentary

Santa Singh is speaking in the tradition of Freud. The Father of Psychology noted the human tendency to regress to the womb in the face of adversity and crisis.

In the aftermath of the financial meltdown and the resultant economic upheaval, the newspapers have been full of reports of so many young men and women unable to find a job or having lost one, all forced to move back in with their parents. Leaving aside the physical element, Santa's analogy is quite correct; parents in this case have had to relive a phase of their lives, one which they had presumed was over and done with.

Unknowingly perhaps, Santa has employed a fitting literary metaphor too. A 'reverse' is an unexpected setback. A series of such setbacks is often spoken of as a 'train of reverses'. A 'reverse gear' elevates this to one continuum of misfortunes.

For Whom the Bell (Does Not) Toll/s

Many years ago, in a less frenetic age where it was normal for friends to drop in unannounced on one another, an old chum from the other side of the town stopped by to pay Banta Singh a visit. Reaching the front door, he rang the doorbell. There was no answer. He waited briefly, then tried ringing the bell again. Still nothing. He looked around and noticed that Banta's scooter was outside the house, which indicated that he should be at home.

The friend tried again, this time holding his finger on the bell button for a while. When there was still no response, he wondered what to do. After pondering a little, he decided to give it one more shot before turning around and heading back home. He stepped back from the door and yelled, 'Oye Bante,' then reached forward and pressed the bell again for good measure. His efforts were rewarded; Banta's face appeared at the window upstairs. Without moving from the window, Banta shouted out to his friend, '*Oye yaara, oh ^&%$^ bell kam ni kardi. Darwaje nu khatkhatayeen* (Old chap, that ^&%$^ bell is out of commission. Try knocking on the door).'

Commentary

Note that it is not 'try knocking on the door next time'. Instead, it is 'try knocking on the door'. Banta wants him to knock on the door so that he can open it *this* time! Knowing that his friend is waiting outside is not enough; Banta has to be duly intimated of this—Through Proper Channel—in the Indo-British bureaucratic lexicon. 'Process over purpose' is the classic hazard of the babudom[2]; an attitude still all too widely prevalent in India.

There is a flip side to it as well. 'Purpose over process'— a response to red tape and official delay—is the origin of a variety of ills, including bribery, shortcuts and other novel forms of jugaad[3] to circumvent rules and nullify safeguards, which frequently end up defeating the purpose itself.

Unfortunately, it is quite possible for a society to have both these tracks—a rigid bureaucracy and a lawless

---

[2] From 'babu' (clerk), a euphemism for a bureaucracy of clerks
[3] An unconventional, often off-the-books, fix

land—both running in parallel, each providing an excellent rationale for the other.

Oye Bell-e Bell-e!

After the friend's visit (in the previous story), Banta was a little embarrassed and decided it was time to have the doorbell fixed. He found an electrician and described the problem to him. Santa Singh (for that was the electrician's name) assured him that for him this was a mere *'khabbe hatth da khel* (a piece of cake)', and promised to stop by the following Sunday. 'It should be no more than a half hour's work,' Santa declared.

All day long, Banta waited and waited. There was no sign of the electrician. When evening fell he was cursing himself for putting his trust in the other's promise, missing thereby his customary Sunday afternoon treat: a visit to the movie theatre followed by the usual s'mose-te-chaat at the sidewalk stall on the way home. On his way to work, on Monday morning, he stopped by the electrician's shop, determined to give him a piece of his mind.

'*Oye ^&%$^, ki hoya kal tainnu? Saara din ^&%$^ tera intejaar karde karde thakk gaya...*(What the devil happened to you yesterday? I was tired waiting for you the whole bloody day...)'

He expected Santa to be contrite and apologetic. What he encountered instead was high indignation. '*Khud gayab te mainnu gaalaan kadd de ho? Kal praa de twaade ^&%$^ bell vajaunde vajaunde rorhe peh gaye ungli'ch* (You yourself were nowhere to be seen, and here you're hurling abuses at me? Brother, I've grown a callus on my finger ringing your blessed doorbell)!'

Commentary

In computer science they call it the deadlock or the deadly embrace. There are several variations to the deadlock problem, all of which involve two independent processes using a shared resource. If the processes somehow are not able to communicate with each other, a situation might arise wherein one process is finished with the resource (either completely or temporarily), but the other is unaware that the resource is available for it to use. Hence, both end up waiting forever for the resource (or at least, all Sunday as in this instance!). The solution to the deadlock is for one process to notify the other. There are numerous systematic techniques by which one can accomplish this. In software jargon one such method is called semaphore, a frightfully unoriginal reuse of an ancient naval notification drill involving flags and dancing sailors to exchange messages between ships.

In this case, one of the solutions could have been for Santa to yell out to Banta (although, judging by the previous joke, who knows where that would have led!). Alternatively, he could've left a note on the door saying that he had come over. As a solution to deadlock, one of the processes (Banta, in this case) could have checked periodically if there was any communication regarding the resource left by the other process (Santa, here). In this scenario, Banta would've found Santa's note and then presumably proceeded to the latter's shop right away to berate him.

The proliferation of cellphones in our times has obviated this particular aspect of the problem. Today's Santa and Banta would both likely be proud possessors of the latest model of an iPhone or Android.

But the fatuousness of the human mind remains unchanged.

Consider this: the Americans went into Iraq claiming that Iraq posed an imminent military threat to its neighbours. The next thing you knew, they were setting up a huge infrastructure to 'train the Iraqi army'!

'Two things are infinite—the universe, and human stupidity,' Einstein is supposed to have remarked, adding, '...and I'm not so sure about the universe.'

Digg'ya K'rraincy, ki Kariye Assi

It had been a tough year for the Indian economy. Prices were rising, economic indicators were pointing resolutely downward. It was all cause for considerable discomfiture to the government of the day, led by Prime Minister Sardar Manmohan Singh. With elections fast approaching, poor economic news was like a vitamin-rich tonic for the political opposition, which lost no time in making the most of the government's predicament. Particularly galling was the fact that Sardar Manmohan Singh was himself a doctorate in economics, a detail those lampooning the administration seldom forgot to work into their punchlines.

And now, capping it all, a yawning current account deficit had become the ostensible cause of a sudden drop in the value of the national currency, the rupee. In just a few days, the Indian rupee had lost nearly a quarter of its value against standard currencies such as the American dollar, the euro, etc., making front page news every day, none of it soothing to the government's ears.

Not that any of this was causing the least bit of intrusion upon the nation's abiding preoccupation—cricket. The fortunes of the Indian team, its losses to England and Pakistan, and its subsequent victories over Australia, all clamoured for, claimed and continued to command a lion's share of the public's attention.

It was in this context that a news reporter found himself unexpectedly sharing an elevator ride with the prime minister. Deciding to avoid the usual political questions, which the latter was notoriously adept at sidestepping, he thought to surprise the PM by asking something completely outside the box.

'Mr Prime Minister, what sports do you like to watch?' he began.

The prime minister gave a big smile, obviously relieved. 'I love to watch cricket, whenever it is played in India.'

The reporter, in true tradition, ventured to probe further.

'But sir, which aspect of the game do you particularly enjoy, batting, bowling, fielding...' he trailed off, wanting to give the prime minister an open-ended choice.

The answer he received stumped him.

'The toss. I like to watch the tossing of the coin.'

And before the journalist could ask 'Why', Dr Manmohan Singh, PhD (Economics) from Cambridge, added dryly, 'It is the only time these days that I see our rupee going up,' as the elevator doors closed behind him.

Commentary

In this story Dr Singh belies the common picture of economists being pessimists and of economics being the 'dismal science'. President Harry Truman once expressed his wish for a one-armed economist, because each one of his economic advisers kept adding, 'But, on the other hand...', after proffering any opinion. Truman was actually setting himself up for disappointment; there are no unalloyed gains in economics, which is why the phrase 'on the other hand...' is practically the 'stock-in-trade' of economists.

The rupee does go up during the toss, but we can be sure that Dr Singh, the student of economics, did not neglect his school physics lessons to such an extent as to be unaware that the same rupee which goes up also comes down. Indeed it would be a strange toss if it didn't, to say nothing of the capital outflows!

The same inevitability seems to hold as much for economics. Currencies, stock prices, interest rates, property values, even economies and nations, elevators...anything that goes up must come down too, and vice versa. Only, many things that happen in an instant in physics happen over time in economics. Monotonic increase or decrease appears to be rare if not nonexistent in our universe, entropy being a well-known exception to the rule. According to cosmologists, even the universe, which is ever expanding, will at some point in the distant future begin to collapse.

Made in Japan

Mr Yasuhiro Tanaka, a wealthy Japanese businessman, was paying his first ever visit to India. He was proud of his country's manufacturing expertise, and never missed an opportunity to point out high-quality Japanese products to anyone within earshot. By the time he had exited the New Delhi airport after clearing the immigration and customs check, he had already noted a dozen things that clearly underlined his country's unmatched superiority, not just in manufacturing but even in soft skill areas such as courtesy, customer service, etc.

Stepping out of the air-conditioned international

terminal into the hot New Delhi summer afternoon, Mr Tanaka was accosted by Banta Singh. They spoke two entirely different languages, but Mr Tanaka understood enough to surmise that the other was asking if he needed a taxi. Soon Banta was loading Mr Tanaka's luggage into the boot of his ancient yellow and black Ambassador, and ushering Mr Tanaka into the backseat. Mr Tanaka had somehow conveyed to Banta Singh that he wanted to reach the Ashoka Hotel, and Banta nodded confidently as he noisily gunned the vehicle into gear.

They made their way along the main road, with the Ambassador rattling and wheezing as it was overtaken by other smoother and sleeker cars, a fact Mr Tanaka felt compelled to point out. 'Ah, see, "made in Japan", very fast,' he said, pointing excitedly as a silver-gray Honda zipped by. He repeated the same thing several times during their journey, pointing to numerous Toyotas, Mazdas, Mitsubishis and Nissans that whizzed past Banta Singh's old jalopy.

It was only when they pulled into the gates of the Ashoka that Mr Tanaka noticed the cab-fare meter. He was truly shocked. It had racked up what seemed like an exorbitant fare for just a few kilometres. The taxi stopped at the front porch of the hotel. Banta Singh got out, went to the back of the car, opened the boot and took out the luggage carefully, carrying it and placing it on the front portico. Meanwhile Mr Tanaka was standing outside next to the taxi, his eyes bulging, staring at the meter as if in a trance. He sensed Banta approaching and turned, jabbing

a finger at the meter. 'So much?' he hissed at Banta Singh.

'Meter, sirjee, varry fast. Oye, it is made in J'pan,' explained Banta with a quiet shake of the head.

Commentary

Two different observations can be made, depending on how one looks at this joke. If the meter was indeed made in Japan, as Banta Singh says, then it does hoist the Japanese gentleman with his own petard. The country that makes fast cars surely can make fast taximeters. Pride goeth before a fall, and whatnot. An alternate, and more interesting, perspective is one of creating real versus phantom value. A car is something you can actually use. It is part of the 'real' economy. The meter, in this context, is really just an accounting device. A parallel can be drawn between economies where real things are manufactured versus those where the attention is predominantly on the amount of creativity in financial and accounting innovations. In his book *Bad Money*, Kevin Phillips, adviser to President Richard Nixon, speaks of how the American economic decline is highlighted by the downgrading of the manufacturing sector and the upgrading of the financial sector.[4] A chart in the book shows this in stark detail: in 1950, 29.3 per cent of the US GDP came from its manufacturing industry, and 10.9 per cent from the financial services. By 2005, this had been turned on its head with 12.0 per cent from manufacturing and 20.4 per cent from financial services.[5]

The lesson is that relying on moneymaking from financial legerdemain cannot sustain a nation for long. Banta's smart comeback is good for a chuckle, but Mr Tanaka does have good reason to bet on the ability to make real/quality stuff.

(En)Countering Sankara

Banta Singh is going for a walk in the forest when, suddenly, he notices his friend Santa Singh come rushing out of the bushes. Santa looks terrified and is acting all desperate.

'Oye Bante, run, run, run quickly. There is a bear,' he

---

[4]*Reckless Finance, Failed Politics, and the Global Crisis of American Capitalism* by Kevin Phillips, Viking, 2008
[5]Ibid., p. 31

says, pointing into the distance, unable to speak, panting for breath.

Banta also begins to run alongside Santa. 'What happened?' he asks Santa.

'I was walking down the path when suddenly I saw this bear,' replies Santa between gasps. 'It growled. To slow it down, I picked up a handful of mud and threw it at its face.' He waits to get his breath back, glancing back at the bear still some distance away.

'Some of it got into the bear's eye and angered it so much that it began chasing me.'

Banta comes to a stop. He appears furious, shouting at Santa, 'Oye ^&%$^, you gave me all this trouble, for what? You threw the mud at the bear. You incited the animal... You run if you want to. Why should I?'

Commentary

There is a well-known story of Adi Sankaracharya. One day when Sankara was walking in a forest along with a disciple, an elephant began chasing them. Sankara and the acolyte both ran for their life and managed to hide safely. Even as they were running, the disciple gently twitted his guru at their fleeing, which appeared to nullify one of his famous teachings, '*Brahman satyam, jagat mithya* (The brahman/universe is true, the material world false).'

'*Kim palaayanam, gajopi mithyam* (Why are we running, after all the elephant is an illusion),' asked the disciple.

To which Sankara is said to have given his celebrated

response, '*Gajopi mithyam, palaayanopi mithyam* (The elephant is illusory, and so too is our running away).'

There is also the story of Androcles, older than that of Sankara, where the lion remembers his long-ago kindness and spares him while killing others. And closer home, Ramana Maharshi, another icon of spirituality, is said to have lived in the presence of tigers and the like, who would come and sit by him as he meditated.

The world may or may not be an illusion, but surely each one of us carries our own understanding that we bring to bear (no pun intended) in our interactions with it. Here, Banta is applying the canons of human society, of wrongdoing and punishment, to the world of the jungle. I have done no wrong, what do I have to fear?

It is a question that everybody grapples with every day. We ponder over it precisely because it eludes a simple answer, or at least, every simple answer turns out to be a non-answer. It is a difficult question because, as with the Sankara story, there are as many answers as the number of assumptions one is prepared to make.

The Hitch-hiker's Guide to the G'laxy

At the roadside dhaba, the debate had somehow wended its way to the relative merits of the various heavenly bodies in the firmament, viewed from a utilitarian perspective. Numerous contenders were considered from astronomical and astrological standpoints both. One by one Mars, Venus, Saturn, etc. all fell by the wayside, until only two of the original contestants remained—the sun and the moon. Here another brisk discussion began. The gathering seemed evenly divided on the issue. Several more rounds of chate-s'mosay (tea and samosas) failed to produce a resolution and there seemed to be no clear winner.

Then Banta Singh, who had all this while remained silent, decided that it was time to speak up and bring matters to a close.

'Vekho ji, daf'nitely the moon is the more useful...,' he began.

Several sun supporters had just opened their mouths to argue, but Banta Singh, having anticipated them, raised his right hand to urge patience and calm. The opponents fell silent.

'Oh yes, I know. Light,' he continued. 'Oye, but just think. The moon gives us light during the night, when we really need it, whereas the sun only shines during the day, when we least require it.'

With that the discussion ended.

Commentary

There are several pieces of insight in this joke. The first is that the most essential ingredients of our lives are free, constant and therefore, subject to blatant disregard by us, often to the extent of derision. The moon, which waxes and wanes, showing us any kind of nocturnal illumination half the month at best, seems more useful than the poor sun which toils away 365 days of the year. Air, sunlight and water, whose very abundance hides their utility, are frequently the objects of our disdain. Their constancy, like that of mother's love, is taken for granted and not even noticed.

The moon, as perhaps Banta Singh did not realize, has no light of its own to offer. It merely reflects the light from the sun. This, too, points at a curious feature of our lives and logic. The messenger is frequently deemed worthier than the source. My late uncle was a wise individual who recognized this paradox, as illustrated by a little story he once shared with me. After his retirement, my uncle and aunt lived with their daughter and her young children. The son-in-law worked in the merchant navy and was therefore travelling abroad most of the time. Efficient and systematic by nature, it fell on my uncle to manage the banking for the household. In this case, it also involved investing the remittances from abroad, etc. This latter feature soon earned him platinum-level service at the bank. One day when the son-in-law was back home between tours of duty, he accompanied my uncle to the bank. As soon as they reached the bank, the staff was all over my uncle, but much to his embarrassment, completely ignored the gentleman who really owned the deposits of which my uncle was merely a manager!

Kin-knee Umar?

An elderly sardar was finding the pain in his left knee quite irksome. It wasn't unbearable, but it was enough to keep him bothering throughout the day. He tried various home remedies, all to no avail. He had resisted going to the specialist, although his children had been urging him for some time now. His sons and daughters did have a point. Rare were conversations with him which did not, within five minutes, veer around to the subject of his left knee. The scales tipped one Sunday afternoon, when his wife abandoned his side and went over to that of their children. It was futile to resist any longer. '*Chal tu ehna chaundi hain tah specialist naal mil laanga* (Okay, if you wish it so much I will see the specialist),' he conceded, with a scowl at his wife. He tossed a glance at his younger son to indicate his capitulation. But not without a final note of defiance, '*Par main hune tuhannu kainna, hona kuchch nee uththe. ^&%$^ speshlist-veshlist kol paihe barbaad karan di khaaj ehni hai tuhannu saareyaan nu, taan main ki karaan* (But I want to tell you right now it's going to be of no use. You're all itching to waste money on a bloody specialist, so what am I to do)?'

The day of the appointment rolled around. The specialist spent an hour with him, putting him through various movement exercises, besides ordering blood and urine tests, x-rays, scans and whatnot. He asked him to come back when the results were in.

At the next appointment, the specialist explained patiently that there was nothing of great concern in the tests. However, it was true that his left knee had undergone some kind of arthritic degeneration which was causing him all this trouble. There was nothing to be done really; active intervention meant some potentially unpleasant trade-offs. He wanted to calm down the old man. Peering over his reading glasses, the specialist smiled, 'Sardarji, after all, that left knee of yours, you have to realize, is 85 years old!' He wanted to lend a cheerful tone to what he had to say. He waited for the reply while the son translated his words to the old man.

The young man explained to his father what the doctor had said. The aged sardar muttered something in response.

The son hesitated briefly. Even when he spoke, it was clear he was not planning to convey his father's words verbatim, only a paraphrase. 'My father says,' he began slowly. A cloud seemed to lift from his face, and he looked like a man who has decided to take the plunge, 'Tell the ^&%$^ specialist that my other knee is also 85 years old, and ask how come it is doing so well!'

Commentary

Two millennia since Galen and nearly a century after penicillin, individual successes and failures with medicines, modern or ancient, appear to be precisely that—individual. Without any prejudice to the remarkable, even astounding, progress in medicine and advances in surgical techniques, there is still much about which doctors are in the dark. Assuming there is nothing obvious in the sardarji's past line of work that could have set in motion such degeneration, it is difficult to pinpoint why this should be so. A further twist emerges from a study done in New York many years ago. When doctors were concluding that back pain was often caused by a particular curvature of the spine, someone thought to check out the spine images of those who did not have back pain. Imagine their surprise when these were quite often found to be just as distorted! Sometimes a similar damage does not translate to similar sensations of pain. There are people who exercise and eat right and end up dropping dead, and others who carouse and ignore every edict of proper care without apparent ill-effect. There seems nothing more inscrutable than our human body.

The sardarji in this story appears to be on to an old and wise adage, 'Into each life some rain must fall'. And yes, to many old people, their ailments are an excellent fodder for conversation, just as fascinating as the latest gadget to the modern-age teenager.

Push-kar Fair (Push It Again)

As Banta Singh was leaving from work one evening, the security guard on duty outside the front gate noticed that he was wheeling away instead of driving his late model Bajaj Chetak motorscooter. *Must be some kind of a vehicle breakdown*, the guard thought to himself.

He called out to Banta, 'Sirjee, any problem with the scooter?'

'Oh, the scooter? Nothing. Why do you ask?' was Banta's reply as he stopped and turned towards the guard.

'But...then...why aren't you riding it?' The guard couldn't help but ask. 'Oh, that. It's because I don't have the key,' Banta replied with a shake of his head.

'Did you drop it somewhere? Sirjee, if you would like, I could help you look for it. My duty ends in just ten minutes,' the guard offered gallantly.

'Oh no, no, no, thanks. It's not lost. I just forgot it at home this morning.'

The guard was not impertinent by nature. But now he could barely contain himself. 'But sirjee, then how did you drive to the office in the morning?'

'Oye kambakhta (you dunderhead), obviously I couldn't drive. I had to wheel it all the way here,' Banta explained patiently.

Commentary

On whatever else opinion might be divided, it will be agreed by all that there was no earthly reason for Banta to be trundling the scooter alongside that day. But then it is always so clear when someone else is engaging in blatant stupidity. All of us have done something similar, however; metaphorically speaking, who does not carry on his shoulders some needless burden or the other? For many it is a matter of show and pomp. They will go to ridiculous lengths to sustain a façade. For others, it is an unthinking activity. Circumstances might change but they continue doing what they have always done. The modern American home has so much junk that just sits and occupies space without providing any utility. The comedian George Carlin had a remarkable piece on this aspect of American life. Like the famous story of the monkey trap, where all that the monkey had to do to escape was to let go of the bait by opening its fingers. Instead, it grips the bait ever more firmly, giving the trapper ample time to come over and capture it. The liberating art of load shedding, if you will, has been learned by very few outside our electricity companies, who, unfortunately, seem to have learnt it rather too well!

MBA or Aīnvay E?

The young man standing across the table from Banta Singh looked smart. He wore a striped suit of dark gray, a pale blue cotton shirt and a pleasing sober crimson tie with a nice blue pattern. A buff leather laptop bag/attaché completed the picture of an executive on a fast upward trajectory.

He had graduated with high honours from a leading business school in the South, and followed it up with a year in a well-known financial firm. He was proud of his achievements and saw no reason to be modest. He had seen Banta Singh's quarter page ad in the newspaper, seeking a general manager of top quality managerial talent and offering a truly attractive pay package. He had absentmindedly sent in a job application, and here he was at the interview. Banta Singh was the company's founder and owner.

The young MBA had been puzzled by what he had seen so far. There was not much online information about the company, so he had to rely on impressions gathered during the hour he had spent being taken around the plant. It seemed to be a workman-like enterprise with not too much by way of frills and fancy. Certainly... But Banta was now saying something.

'Oye, sitdown, puttar, sitdown.'

He reached across to shake hands and gestured towards the chair. An assistant brought in coffee and biscuits. After taking a sip, Banta began, 'So, what did you think? All my people who spoke to you today really like you. I'm not going to ask any questions, but I'm here to answer all the questions you might have.'

True to his first-class training, the young man did not waste his time with uhs and ums. 'Sir, why did you want to hire a general manager?'

Banta shook his head, his face breaking into a broad smile. 'Excellent question! I will tell you. For nearly twenty years I have done nothing but worry about this company.

Now I want to relax and let someone else to take over the worrying!' he replied.

Taking this as his cue, the MBA took Banta through a gruelling course of questions about the company. Banta's responses only served to confirm his earlier apprehensions; they could scarcely afford to stay in business, let alone afford somebody like him. He was quite disgusted and ready to let the old man have it.

'With all due respect, sir, I can't imagine why you even called me. You know the salary I want, the BMW and driver I would expect, a luxury apartment companies give people like me, plus the domestic staff, chef, vacation package, etc. Now, how do you think your company is going to get the money for all that?'

Banta smiled again. 'That, puttar,' he said, 'will be your first worry as GM.'

Commentary

Absurd as it may seem, viewing it in proper perspective tells us it is not at all far-fetched. The young business executive appears more concerned about his perks than the business he would have to run. This is, actually, a very good insight into the kind of potential he might have. A workplace can be broadly divided into two kinds of people—employees and owners. An employee's mentality is one of doing the job and drawing a salary. The owner's mentality goes far beyond; the owner is one who just cannot leave the job behind at the end of the day—he lies awake all night agonizing over it. Not about losing it, for that is the employee's mindset. The owner worries about what needs to be done.

The key difference is captured in one word that Banta used—worry. Curiously, this has nothing to do with one's position within an organization. A person at the very bottom may bring everything he has to the job; while a board chairman could be expending all his energy persuading the board to grant him a bonus even when the company is awash in red ink.

The essence of all this is expressed in the words said by President Kennedy in his inaugural address, 'Ask not what your country can do for you; ask what you can do for your country.'

A Fitting Choice?

Banta Singh was sitting at a tea stall, sipping from the saucer into which he had poured piping hot tea from the cup. His friend Santa had not shown up for their usual afternoon get together at the tea shop. After waiting for more than an hour, he called Santa's cellphone. There was no response. And so he decided to order the usual tea and bread-pakora for himself. He was musing absently, when he heard a heavy engine noise. Looking up, he saw a spanking new red Corvette coming to a halt outside the tea stall. He was not the only one to rush outside to investigate. It was not every day that a fancy set of wheels showed up at the rundown adda.

What followed next was nothing short of astounding. Santa Singh hopped out of the Corvette, smiled a big smile, walked towards Banta and said, 'My new car, how do you like it?'

There was a huge hubbub with everybody asking questions at the same time. Somebody suggested they go in and sit down so they could all hear the full story. When they were all settled inside with tea and pakoras in front of them, Santa began his story.

'I was walking along the street to come here, when this beautiful girl in her twenties, dressed in kurta and jeans, pulled up next to me in this red sports car,' he

began. Every man in the tea stall leaned forward so as not to miss anything.

'She tossed a beautiful smile at me and said, "Sardarji, I am new to this town and I think I've lost my way. Can you get into the car and show me how to get to my uncle's place?"' Santa continued.

'Then what happened?' somebody from the audience inquired eagerly.

'Before I knew it, this car had already gathered high speed, and we were outside the town limits and into the countryside.'

'My God! Then? Then?' The audience was agog.

'Then she turned at a side road and we kept driving until we reached a deserted grove. I kept protesting, saying, "What are you doing? Where are you taking me?" But by that time she had stopped under a clump of trees. Then... she got out of the car, ran to the front and slowly, started to take off her clothes!'

The excitement in the tea stall was palpable.

'I couldn't believe my eyes. This beautiful girl was standing in front of me, stark naked, throwing her clothes onto a low branch of a tree nearby.'

The collective heartbeat of the audience could have rivalled the dhuk-dhuk-dhuk of the Corvette's engine.

'She smiled demurely at me, then she tossed her head slightly to one side, making her tresses cascade as if they were a waterfall. Then...she gave me a sly wink and whispered, "Sardarji, take whatever you want."'

Cries of 'Ooye, ooye, ooye', drowned the room as the

audience, eyes tightly shut to imagine better, expressed its collective feeling.

'*Taan tu ki keeta, oye* (Then what did you do)?' came a voice from the front row, breaking the spell. This was Banta Singh speaking.

A derisive laughter swept the room. Was there even a need to ask, was the consensus. Evidently there was, for Santa was replying.

'*Main tah ^&%$^ sidda gaddi chukki te natth piya* (I just picked the bloody car and sped away).'

Banta nodded his head in approval as he slapped his friend on the back. '*Oye Sante, tu bilkul changa keeta oye. Vaise vih ohde kapde tainnu aane vi ni si* (Hey Santa, you did absolutely the right thing! In any case, her clothes would have never fitted you).'

Commentary

Let us for a moment put aside the obvious import of the joke, which is, that Santa (and Banta) was impervious to the meaning of the girl's all too evident overtures.

The real humour of the joke lies in its universality. In our own lives very often each one of us is missing the bus by choosing the safe option instead of the venturesome one—'calculation over caprice'. Santa's choice brings to light the nature of conventional wisdom, whereas Banta's is even more conservative—caution rules. Yet, as one grows older, it looks as if the only things worth doing were the things one ought never to have done. T.S. Eliot captured

this beautifully in his poem 'The Waste Land':
The awful daring of a moment's surrender.
Which an age of prudence can never retract.
By this, and this only, we have existed.

We are taught by parents, family and society alike to be prudent, which is to say, opt always on the side of accumulation. Most of us thus have no idea what 'abandon', as in joy, means. Abandon, as in letting go, becomes a lost art, as does the experience of joy.

Statute of Limitations

The conversation had turned to sensational childhood events.

Santa: '*Jadon main nikka si ik vaari dooji manjil toh digg piya si* (When I was a kid I once fell down from the second floor)!'

Banta: '*O ^&%$^... Kidre jaan-waan tah ni gayi* (Holy smoke... Hope you didn't lose your life or something)?'

Santa: '*Muddat di gal eh, pra. Hunn theek-theek yaad vi ni mainnun* (Happened ages ago, brother. Now even I don't remember all the details).'

Commentary

The joke is a brilliant illustration of Orwellian doublespeak by using an obviously absurd example. Of course, if someone sitting across from you is talking about his childhood accident, clearly he survived it. This conversation of the absurd, a patently ridiculous question which receives an even more preposterous answer, is, yet, a daily feature of our lives. World leaders speak routinely of peace while building and buying armaments in hundreds of billions of dollars. Experts discuss the environment in grave tones of anxiety on TV shows underwritten by the very companies that are turning pristine corners of the earth into ecological hellholes. One has only to pay attention to discover one's own disconnect. By poking fun at themselves, Santa and Banta are merely pointing out our own 'emperor's new clothes'.

Siddī sī Gal[6]

The neighbour had been watching the strange goings-on for a good two hours. He had been drawn, at first, by the noise from the backyard next door. The medley of growls, yelps and menacing barks, interspersed with human cries of pain and choicest Punjabi oaths would have piqued the interest of a far more incurious individual; and this neighbour was a journalist after all. The sight that greeted

---

[6]Translation: a straightforward matter

him, when he peered over the fence, was nothing short of remarkable. He forgot all about the half-eaten breakfast on his dining table as he gaped in frank disbelief.

Banta Singh seemed to be attempting to insert the tail of his pet dog into a metal pipe. The altercation was because of the dog taking strong exception to Banta Singh's endeavours. It would be a hard enough task for three people; Banta was trying it single-handed. Time after time he would succeed in calming the animal enough to settle down near him, but the moment he lifted the tail, the dog would snap, draw its teeth, snarl and finally bite Banta's hand, eliciting some high-flown abuse. Once every ten times or so, he would actually manage to get a little bit of the tail into the pipe before the dog got wise and shook it off.

The neighbour couldn't believe what he was seeing. An adage is something one uses as a metaphor; seldom does one expect to see it enacted literally. And yet...here the journalist went off on a reverie, mentally composing the headline he would give to his article. He realized that, as a serious professional, he could scarcely write the piece without talking to its principal character. He hailed Banta, who had been so engrossed as to not notice him before. Banta got up and walked towards the fence to talk to him. 'Can you actually straighten a dog's tail?' the journalist asked him gently.

Banta looked at his neighbour with a tinge of pity. '*Lo ji kamaal karde ho tussi vi. Oye, main sochya tussi aidde vadde journa-list ho, parhe likhe* (Hey, you surprise me. And

I thought you were a big journalist, well read). Don't you know even the Holy Book says, "*Suaan poochh na soodho* (A dog's tail cannot be straightened)"? Pardon me, but what a ridiculous question!'

The journalist was a little taken aback by this harangue. He said, frostily, 'Sardarji, I too know the proverb. What, then, have you been trying to accomplish for the last two hours?'

Banta Singh shook his head. 'Oye bewaqoofa, I am trying to bend the pipe,' he explained with a sad smile.

Commentary

The encounter between the intellectual and the doer has rarely been better showcased. It brings to mind a famous saying of George Bernard Shaw, 'The reasonable man tries to adapt himself to the world. The unreasonable man persists in trying to make the world adapt to him. Therefore, all progress depends on the unreasonable man'. The rules expert has all the reasons why something cannot be done. The doer is looking at the problem from a different standpoint entirely.

Bill ki Baatein Kahi Nahin Jaati[7]

In the heart of New Delhi stands an 18th century observatory, Jantar Mantar. It was built by Maharaja Jai Singh, a keen astronomer. It has always been a city landmark, a quaint anachronism of strange-looking structures in pink and white, nestled amidst modern high-rise offices and shopping complexes. In the last few decades it has also become New Delhi's Hyde Park, the standard venue for protest gatherings.

It was in this latter context that the ancient observatory became the centre of national attention a few years ago. It was here that the anti-corruption agitators, led by Anna Hazare, staged their dharna (sit-in). Anna himself had camped there, on an indefinite fast, demanding that the Union Government enact without delay a law on curbing corruption.

Banta Singh worked in one of the office buildings close by. It was his habit to take a short walk during the lunch hour, terminating at the roadside chole-bhature stall across the street from Jantar Mantar. As he stood enjoying his lunch, he could hear the slogans raised by Anna's supporters, high both in enthusiasm and decibels. Casual inquiry among his fellow eaters told him that this man,

---

[7]Original: *dil ki baatein kahi nahin jaati*. With apologies to Mir Taqi Mir

Anna, was on a hunger strike. His face assumed a puzzled expression, although he remained silent. A few days later, while he stood eating lunch, across the street Anna Hazare was giving an impassioned speech, demanding that the legislation be passed immediately. Banta Singh could bear it no longer. '*Eh banda khule aam public da bewaqoof banaunda piya* (This fellow is openly making a fool of the public),' he expostulated, much to the consternation of the other customers. He pushed on, '*Oye, mainnu ik gal dusso. Jeh sachi p'uhka hai tah bill kis layi mang riha hai* (Tell me something. If he has really not eaten, why is he asking for the bill)?'

Commentary

George Orwell began his obituary of Gandhi with the words, 'Saints should always be judged guilty until they are proved innocent'. Banta Singh applies the same measure to Anna Hazare, and finds him falling short. If Gandhi was called half a politician and half a saint, Hazare, a self-styled Gandhian, may be justifiably viewed as 10 per cent politician, 5 per cent saint and 150 per cent grouch. A good man and all that, but something doesn't add up, is how he is often seen. The disquiet about Hazare that many people sense but few can place precisely, Banta seems to have managed to capture rather well in this imaginary tale.

The VIP

Passengers on the Amritsar–Delhi train were getting ready for an afternoon snooze when there was a sudden sizzle of apprehension in the compartment. Whispers of, '*TTE aaya hai* (The Traveling Ticket Examiner is here),' were making their way from the front cabin to the back. Anybody who has travelled the Indian Railways will recall the tiny pang of anxiety that sets off a rising panic upon hearing these words. Even if the tickets are perfectly in order, a momentary parade of questions—whether they are safe, not forgotten at home, or accidentally lost to a pickpocket and other such doubts—cycles through one's brain. Instinctively, travellers pull out their wallets, purses, etc., rifle through and extract their tickets, their faces registering a metamorphosis from tense to relaxed upon finding what they are looking for. They are now ready for the brief ordeal, during which the TTE takes their documentation, scans it with a solemn face, then checks the names and ages against the passenger list, glances back at them to verify if the age and sex match, before handing over the tickets with an unsmiling 'I'll-let-you-go-this-time' manner, and then raises his eyebrows at the next passenger to demand his or her ticket.

And here was Banta Singh, travelling without a ticket. He had already tried the usual ruse from 'Ticketless Travel 101', locking oneself in one of the bathrooms, but had found those precincts occupied by people in more genuine need. And, each moment, the TTE, with a nameplate reading, 'Santa Singh', was drawing closer and closer. Banta racked his brains for a way out. He was on his way to a business meeting in Delhi, and was dressed in a fine-looking suit and tie. He decided to press home this sartorial advantage; brazen it out as he had seen one of the characters do in a recent film.

It was at this point that TTE Santa Singh gently tapped him on the shoulder and said, 'Ticket, please.'

Banta was ready. *'Ticket? Ticket! Oye, tainnu pataa vi hai tu kidde naal gal kar riha hain* (Do you even know who you're speaking to)?' he said, sounding angry and insulted.

Santa was really taken aback. A diligent and sincere employee he certainly was, but he had no illusions of heroism. Who could it be? *'Haanji* (Yes, sir),' he said softly, letting his voice trail.

Banta was not a man to play for small stakes. Nothing but the best. If you were going to pretend to have patrons, why reach but among the most famous in the land? *'Sonia Gandhi da kaddi naan suniya hai?* (Ever heard the name Sonia Gandhi)?' he said gravely in a low, even voice, his demeanour radiating confidence.

He was silently praying, hoping that the other would believe what he had to say next, that he was Soniaji's private secretary, when he found that Santa was no longer to be seen. Glancing down he noticed the TTE touching his feet.

Santa straightened up. Shaking his head, he said, *'Ajj tak sirf naan suniya si, vekhya kaddi ni si* (Till today I had only heard the name, but had never seen),' he said, his voice trembling with reverence, before turning to roust out a sitting passenger so the VIP could take a seat.

Commentary

Context is everything. Each communication relies on an underlying context. Much of the humour beneath our jokes consists of a misunderstood or misplaced context. Leaving aside for a moment the question of whether VIPs should be allowed to get away with travelling ticketless, the fact that Sonia Gandhi was a lady should have given away Banta immediately. In such situations a kind of common knowledge is expected regardless. Curiously enough, this is at times found lacking even in the most advanced countries. Highly trained individuals, confronted with the slightest step outside their immediate domain, become near-ignoramuses. To Santa Singh's credit, he had at least heard of Ms Sonia Gandhi, even if he did not know that she wasn't a sardar!

No Double Faulting in This Court

'Banta Singh, Banta Singh, Banta Singh,' the bailiff called out loudly. Banta rose slowly, as did the policemen sitting next to him, and all made their way towards the front of the courtroom. The guard stood outside as Banta mounted the two steps and entered a small enclosure, which was the stand for the accused.

The prosecutor approached Banta, a bound book in his hands. He cast a confident glance at the judge, then addressed Banta Singh in a dramatic tone.

'*Ais Gita te hatth rakh ke kaho ki sach de siwa kuchh nee kahoge* (Place your hand on this Gita and say that you will only speak the truth).'

A suspicious smile came over Banta's countenance. Shaking his head, he replied, '*Oye, tainnu main koi ullu najar aunda haan? Pehle ik Sita te hatth la'an da iljaam pa ke kacheri tak khich ke lai aaya. Hun koyi Gita'ch hatth pa ke dooje case'ch phasaan di koshish karda piya* (Do I look like an idiot to you? First you drag me to court on a false charge of laying my hands on some Sita. Now you want to embroil me in another case by forcing me to touch some Gita).'

Commentary

Entrapment is a well-known device of prosecutions everywhere in the world, and Banta is rightly leery—no pun intended—of what the adversary is trying to pull in the courtroom.

In a more limited sense, the prosecutor's words are less confusing in English. 'Place your hand on the Gita' has a very different connotation than, 'place your hand on Gita'. But the use of the definite article, 'the', has a long and tortuous history, particularly so in Punjab. Many wags attribute the use of the term, 'the Punjab', often used to refer to the geographical region, to Punjabi English playing fast and loose with 'the', frequently found as a prefix to proper nouns! Thus, had the prosecutor used nothing but the Queen's own English, it might not have made the slightest difference to Banta.

Banta Recites the Mahabharata

'*Ik si Kunti* (Once there was a Kunti).'
'*Ohde panj puttar si* (She had five sons).'
'*Ik da naan si P'ihm* (One was called Bhim).'
'*Ik uhdda vadda pra* (One his older brother).'
'*Ik da naan main p'uhl gaya* (One's name has slipped my mind).'
'*Te ik'hore si, te ik'hore si* (And there was another one, and another one).'

Commentary

There you have it, Vyasa's epic (length estimated anywhere between 8000 and 1,00,000 verses depending on what sections are included), reduced to practical proportions by Banta Singh.

But the larger accomplishment here lies in the glissando of communication. In saying, 'One's name has slipped my mind,' Banta makes out that he was doing fine until now, lulling the listener into pretending that he had not forgotten the previous name! The concluding sentence puts the seal on the 'all-is-well' subtext. He has remembered precisely one name out of the five, while gently admitting to only one error explicitly. The plea bargaining lawyers representing the big banks of America could take his correspondence course.

Banta is not being entirely original, though. The use of the technique can be found in as weighty a piece of craftsmanship as the song, 'Do Re Me', from the 1965 super-hit musical, *The Sound of Music,*

...

Sew, a needle pulling thread
La, a note to follow Sew

...

To their credit, the writers of this song used this subterfuge for only one of the seven notes. Banta just went ahead, boldly expanding and improving upon their tentative attempts.

La Place Transforms?

Banta was at the airport with his friend, Bachittar Singh. They were waiting for Banta's brother, who had been in Canada for the last twenty years and was returning to India for the first time. Now, these were the days before cameras were commonplace, to say nothing of smart phones, Instagram, Facebook, etc. Over the two decades, Banta and his brother had kept up a steady correspondence, but no photographs had ever changed hands.

They were watching from the visitor's gallery as the plane landed. Banta could scarcely contain his excitement, as one by one, the passengers began to emerge and step on to the portable stairway that had been wheeled along the tarmac to the door of the plane.

An hour later, the last passenger had exited the aircraft, and Banta had still not spotted his brother. He turned to Bachittar, slapping his forehead as he exclaimed, 'Oye rubba, rubba, twenty years in valaiyat (foreign land). Pra ji (respected brother) must have changed so much. How in the world did I think I was going to recognize him? Let's go downstairs and wait outside so that he can see me.'

Bachittar considered the matter briefly, and discovered another aspect of the problem. 'For that matter, oye Banteya, after twenty years, how is he going to recognize you?' he wondered aloud.

Banta was exasperated. 'Oye bewaqoofa (numbskull), why should that be a problem? *Main kadi valaiyat thodi na gaya si* (As if I ever went abroad)!? I've been right here in Amritsar all the time!'

Commentary

The explanation probably lies in something simple, such as the brother having missed his flight. Still, the joke brings up a couple of interesting issues, one from a conventional standpoint and the other a bit more relativistic (nothing to do with brotherhood though).

People do change when they have lived abroad for long. It is the complaint of many NRIs visiting India that, despite their dress and speech being identical to that of the locals, shopkeepers and other vendors appear to somehow know they are from abroad, and jack up the prices accordingly! Often the change is in subtle aspects, hard to pinpoint but noticeable overall. Recently, I heard the story of an Indian from abroad at a south Delhi marketplace, where the shopkeeper had indicated he knew this person did not live in India. Pressed to explain what had given him away, the shopkeeper sheepishly pointed out how the outsider had taken care to use the trashcan, instead of throwing his garbage on the ground as per the local custom.

There is in 'Special Relativity' the paradox of the identical twins, one of whom stays on earth while the other takes off on a rocket moving close to the speed of light. When the travelling twin returns, it is found that the twin on earth has aged more compared to the other! Even though his near relative had travelled far, it was in distance and not in time, and Banta had it wrong when he thought he would have changed little compared to his brother. Nonetheless, his instinct that one would change relative to the other appears to be in line with modern physics!

Then there is the entire discourse of psychological time and its effects. The amount of change one encounters affects a huge alteration in one's personality, outlook and even one's physical aspects. Here again, Banta is on the mark.

Inderpreet (Interpret) Singh

Banta's little son Inderpreet, aged just under a year, was a delightful baby, a source of infinite joy to his parents. Banta doted on the toddler, and spent every minute of his spare time cooing and babbling at the little fellow. The child was just beginning to form words, all of them incomprehensible, but to Banta they were the sweetest sounds in the world, bar none.

One day one of his friends had come over to his house, and he noticed that Banta was not only engaged in an earnest babble conversation with the baby, but was also taping the entire exchange. When he got a moment, he pulled Banta aside and asked him why he was recording everything.

'Oye, when he grows up, I will play it again and ask him what he was saying, and more importantly, what I was saying,' Banta replied.

Commentary

A phenomenal joke! It is said that our lack of ability to recall early childhood memories is nature's way of protecting us from the series of painful and traumatic experiences it entails. Beginning with the shock of birth, all the way through a journey full of vicious turns including vaccination, the first bath and being left alone in a crib—the list is long. Early childhood is also the time of greatest peace, safety and comfort, whose memories too are suppressed along with its traumas; this is the price we pay for sanity.

Now, Banta Singh proposes to ask his son, after he reaches a suitable age, what his baby babble means. By his question, he is addressing the heart of language itself. Think about the import of Banta Singh's plan. It implies that the baby knows what it is talking about; only its adult listeners do not understand because they do not know baby language. When the baby grows up and has learned the adult tongue, why not use the latter to interpret the other language (babble) the baby used to speak? It is easy and logical when the languages involved are all adult—after all, this is how interpreters go about their work—they are fluent in more than one language. The problem here is that baby language appears to transform into that of the adult's; the latter is built by discarding the former, somewhat like the butterfly coming into being by the caterpillar going out of existence.

Banta Singh is betting on a different model; that there is a 'program' in the baby's brain that is outputting the 'data' which is the babble. If the grown brain is able to somehow retrieve the old program and decode it, we might be able to make sense of the old babble output. As we understand more and more about the brain—not just of humans but that of dogs, dolphins and migratory birds also—there is every reason to believe that previously inarticulate communications will suddenly begin to acquire a great deal of meaning.

The Last Word

A colleague had asked Banta Singh, if he was free to come over for dinner on Friday evening. Banta accepted, naturally. He had no reason to suspect that this was no innocent invitation. The colleague and his wife lived on the 35th story of a downtown apartment complex.

He detested Banta, and had no intention to host a

pleasant party. He had picked this particular evening, knowing fully well that all the elevators in the building were going to be disabled for maintenance service from 5 p.m. to 10 p.m. that day.

When Banta reached the premises, carrying a bottle of wine for the occasion, the concierge on the ground floor told him of the elevators, and also that he vaguely recalled seeing the hosts go out earlier. The concierge tried calling, but there was no answer from the colleague's home. Banta decided to take a chance, and skipped up the stairs, a couple of steps at a time.

It was a summer evening, and the air was humid. The sports jacket he wore began to get uncomfortable as he reached the 15th floor. Still, he kept going until, sweating and out of breath, he reached the colleague's front door. He stopped to gather his breath for a full 10 minutes before he looked up and rang the doorbell. There was no answer. Nobody was home—the colleague and his wife were out of the town. It was then that Banta noticed a little card stuck along the door frame. It read, 'Sorry, Banta, sudden change of plans. Apologies.' It was only when he absentmindedly opened the card that the perfidy of it all dawned on him. For there it was on the inside, laid out plain in black and white, 'Hope the climb wasn't too bad. Gotcha, sucker!' With a grinning smiley added.

Banta was shocked and devastated, but only briefly. He thought a little, then slowly took out his fountain pen, unscrewed the lid, and began to write slowly in the space below the 'nasty' message on the inside of the card. When he was done, he put the card back exactly the way he had found it. His addition read, 'The joke's on you! I couldn't make it tonight, sudden change of plans.'

He had just gone down one flight of stairs when he had a brain wave. He climbed back up, grabbed the card from the door hinge. He tore off the inner flap of the card, on which he had written earlier, and put it in his pocket. He took out his pen once more and wrote on the front of the card, right below the host's apology, 'No problem. Some other time. Enjoy the wine!–Banta'. Adding a smiley at the end, he placed the card under the bottle of wine he had brought, then skittered down the stairs with a broad grin on his face.

Commentary

During the tensest days of the Cuban Missile Crisis of 1962, the American side received two seemingly contradictory messages from the Soviet. One was entirely belligerent, the other somewhat more conciliatory. President Kennedy and his team chose to ignore the former and instead responded to the latter. In many accounts of those times, this choice, for which there was no logical defence, is viewed as making the difference—between a peaceful resolution of the impasse, and a massive catastrophe.

In human relations, the temptation to have the last word is frequently the cause of grief in the long run. Further, in our day, with tweets, SMSes and emails, the tools to be nasty—and quickly so—all stand so readily at hand. Banta's original message is of course the punchline of the joke, but no less a comment on our actions on that account. The capacity for self-injury in the quest for a smart repartee, seems universal. In this context, Mark Twain's famous saying is worth bearing in mind, 'Always do right. This will gratify some people and astonish the rest'. In either case it can only bring benefits in the long run.

What Banta did ultimately would succeed in blunting his colleague as no amount of crafty one-upmanship ever could. For, his accomplishment was to raise the game to a different class. Even speaking cynically, there is nothing sweeter than a moral victory.

Zero Error Is Not the Same as No Error

'In the morning, I bring you five rabbits. Then, in the afternoon I bring you three more. Come evening, I give you two more rabbits.' The village schoolteacher was addressing the math class. He surveyed his students till his eye alighted upon Banta Singh sitting in the last row.

'*Oye Bante, hun kinne khargosh hone ge tere kol* (So, Banta, and now how many rabbits will you have with you)?'

'*Sirjee, baraan* (Sir, twelve),' came the answer.

The teacher was annoyed, but decided to give the pupil another chance. He posed the same question with progressively smaller numbers, receiving in each instance an answer two more than the correct one. In frustration, he finally reduced it to one, one and one.

'Five,' declared Banta, with no seeming discomfiture.

The teacher took out his cane. After a few swift swishes had landed on the pupil's back, he asked Banta Singh to explain how it was that he was always off by two.

'Sirjee, we already have two rabbits at home,' the lad blurted out through his tears.

Commentary

One of the first topics in practical physics is measurement, and one of the earliest concepts to be discussed is that of the zero error. Simply stated, this reminds you that the readings from the instrument you are using might need to be corrected in light of a misaligned initial setting. I had a friend who would deliberately mess around with the weighing scale in the guest bathroom. It was not at zero when there was no weight on it, and watching the expression on the guest's face as he or she emerged from the restroom provided an ample source of entertainment.

The phrasing of questions, setting the context in particular, is vital in getting the correct answer. Banta was obviously comfortable with additions, but the schoolmaster was still struggling with how to set a problem!

Tiger by the Tail Light

Pandemonium had descended upon the zoo. A strapping tiger in its prime had slipped through the safety measures around its enclosure and was now roaming the precincts wild.

As a senior zoo patrol man, Banta Singh, along with his assistant Santa Singh, was assigned to track and tranquilize the animal.

The duo lost no time in getting into the official Jeep, a ramshackle affair, and setting off in pursuit of the tiger. Santa was riding (tranquilizer) shotgun, while Banta did the driving. They checked various likely locations, but without success. Then, suddenly, as their Jeep had slowed to a crawl so as not to miss their quarry, there was a sudden rush from some thick vegetation alongside the pathway.

A giant roar announced that the tiger was in no mood for trifles. Matching action to sound, it commenced by trying to leap onto their vehicle. It was only by gunning the engine into the next gear and a simultaneous slamming of the gas pedal that they managed to throw off the tiger from the rear. Nothing deterred, the beast raced along close behind as Banta attempted to coax the ancient jalopy into the higher realms of speed. It was a delicate exercise; too much urging could cause the vehicle to break down altogether, with results too ghastly to contemplate.

At this juncture, with the tiger less than two feet behind the Jeep, they saw a fork in the road. Santa exclaimed, '*Oye Bante, ais taranh kareen, khabbe hathh da singal daveen, te gaddi nu sajje passeyon langha layeen. ^&%$^ nu dafaa kariye* (Hey Banta, tell you what, turn on the left indicator, but take the right fork. The ^&%$^ will get lost).'

Banta did as suggested. The tiger was misled and went down the path on the left. They were finally out of danger. But fate intervened once more. The two roads that had diverged were joined together again a few hundred feet later. Sure enough, the tiger was tailing them once more.

A wild, desperate idea entered into Banta's head, and he decided to give it a try. Putting his hand out, he slowed down slightly and moved a little to the side, indicating with his palm that the party behind should overtake.

It turned out to be an absolute stroke of genius. The tiger raced on ahead, giving Santa the view required to fire a tranquilizing dart. This he did, and to cut a long story short, by that evening the tiger was back safely in its enclosure, and Banta and Santa Singh were celebrities featured on every broadcast channel.

But the key question before us remains. What is the moral of this story?

Answer: there are sardars among tigers also...

Commentary

...and rather smart ones, too, going by the looks of it.

The art of withdrawal is one of the most difficult tactics in war. The military academies of the world provide specialized courses in how to conduct a systematic and organized retreat. Getting into a scrape is a cinch compared to getting out of it. The whole episode of Abhimanyu in the Mahabharata deals with precisely this topic. Many crises in the world persist for the sole reason that although the antagonists desire to cease fighting, they just do not know how to go about it.

They can only get deeper and prolong the agony; they do not have any inkling how to get out of the entanglement. Even the concept of surrender has a hoary provenance in India; does the name Vibheeshana of Ramayana ring a bell? This inability to reverse one's course is frequently noticed in young children—many start crying and continue to cry long after the real reason for crying has been addressed!

And here is this brilliant tiger. There is every likelihood that it will be killed. Any foray into the general population would seal its fate. It picks precisely the right agency to provoke, knowing that a tranquilizer dart is vastly to be preferred over a bullet. We can see now that its entire aim was to get in front of Banta and Santa so that it could resume its accustomed life; after all, it was most probably by accident and not design that it escaped. Only, it took a lot of effort to manipulate the duo into acceding to its scheme.

Equalisingh

It was his first ever visit to an establishment of the sort, but Banta Singh was having a fine evening at the strip bar. Enjoying the sight of buxom females in progressive states of undress, as he himself went through a succession of scotch-and-soda orders from the bar, it is fair to say that Banta was in a happy state of mind when one of the strippers came by his table, to thank him for the applause he had been sending her way all evening. A savvy practitioner of the art of persuasion, she knew how a few well-chosen words could result in a substantial tip from a customer in an advanced state of inebriation.

'Howdy, sugar?' She leaned over the table to Banta

and whispered in a low voice, 'Everything going okay?'

Banta nodded vigorously, a nervous excitement coursing through his veins.

'Did I make you happy?' the lady went on, now sitting at the edge of the table, one foot resting on the armrest of his chair. Banta was near delirium, vigourously nodding his head in assent.

She bent forward to bring her face close to his ear and purred rather than spoke, 'Now, mister, can you make me happy?'

Banta considered this question for a full minute. Then he rose and, bestowing upon the stripper the sweetest smile, stepped away from the table. Next, body swaying in perfect time to the music, he slowly proceeded to take off his clothes.

Commentary

George Bernard Shaw on the Golden Rule: 'Do not do unto others as you would that they should do unto you. Their tastes may not be the same'.[8]

---

[8]'Maxims for Revolutionists' from *Man and Superman: A Comedy and a Philosophy* by George Bernard Shaw, 1903

Baptisingh

Banta Singh had moved recently to a small Canadian town, and rented a nice home in a predominantly Catholic neighbourhood. It was a close-knit community, tended by the highly popular local parish priest, Father O'Shaughnessy. They welcomed Banta into their midst, doing their best to make him feel at home.

Things were going really well for some time. It was only when Banta came across a backyard BBQ grill on sale at the store that matters took an unexpected turn. Bringing the grill home, setting it up in his back patio, firing it up, all these were matters of pride to the new immigrant; proof that he was settling into the proper identity. Every Friday afternoon thereafter, his experiments with masala chicken, lamb, fish, etc., grew from strength to strength. The wafting aroma of tasty dishes permeated the entire neighbourhood. Normally, this could only occasion praise and acclaim, but the timing was a problem. Friday was a day of abstinence from meat in the community. A difficult enough ordeal for men and women who relished their food, it was rendered torturous by the afternoon smell of exotic meat concoctions emanating from Banta Singh's backyard. Several of the neighbours brought up the matter with Father O'Shaughnessy, though nobody ever directly said anything to Banta for fear of offending him somehow.

The priest considered everything he had heard and reflected deeply. One evening a couple of months later, Banta's doorbell rang. 'May I come in?' asked Father O'Shaughnessy. Banta welcomed his guest into his living room. Slowly, the father brought up the issue of living among one's neighbours and the broader importance of assimilation. None of this was anathema to Banta Singh. So it was, the following Sunday, that Banta Singh received communion at the church.

As the joyous initiation ceremony in which the entire community participated came to a close, Father O'Shaughnessy sprinkled water from a silver chalice on Banta three times, intoning each time, 'Ye were a Sikh, but from now you are Catholic.' As Banta took leave of him at the end of the baptism, the Father drew him aside and told him about some dos and don'ts of his new faith, including the 'no meat on Fridays' rule.

For about a month, there was peace and happiness in the neighbourhood. Then one day, on a bright Friday afternoon, the smell of masala chicken once again filled the air, emanating from...where else but the Banta Singh residence! Eventually a bunch of neighbours, headed by Father O'Shaughnessy, made their way to Banta's backyard to investigate this recidivist trend.

The sight they beheld robbed them of speech. On a sizzling grill were pieces of spicy chicken. Standing over the apparatus was Banta Singh, sprinkling water on individual cuts as he addressed each of them, 'Oye, you were chicken leg but from now you are corn. Oye, you were chicken

wing but from now you are onion. Oye, you were chicken breast but from now you are potato.'

Commentary

An extraordinary illustration of a common human fallacy—the belief that objective reality, particularly human behaviour, can be changed by renaming things.

In Tamil Nadu, the government has long attempted every cosmetic device to do away with the caste system. One of its most curious innovations in this department was erasing any connection with caste on (even well-known) road signs. For example, 'CP Ramaswamy Aiyar Road' became 'CP Ramaswamy Road'. Of course, there were practical issues, including one where there was a 'Thandavaroya Mudali St' and a 'Thandavaroya Gramani St' not far from each other, both of which ended up becoming 'Thandavaroya Street'! As ridiculous was the turning of 'Dr Nair Road' into a mere 'Dr Road', because Nair indicates a caste (as do Aiyar, Mudali and Gramani).

Decades after these revolutionary makeovers, Tamil Nadu remains second to none in the matter of caste affiliation and consciousness where both are thriving and flourishing.

As the saying goes, you can take the boy out of the country, but not the country out of the boy. Banta Singh proved it, literally.

Oye, Sin nu Ki?

This story is from a few years after the previous joke. The sprinkling episode was now a distant memory, brought up, if ever, only to rib Banta in good fun. To say nothing of integrating into the community, Banta was actually well along the ecclesiastical path, the right hand of Father O'Shaughnessy at the church. The priest thought no end of his assistant, and was keen to teach him every aspect of his work so that one day this sincere young man might take his place.

Currently Banta Singh was absorbing the intricacies of the confessional booth. He was sitting with Father

O'Shaughnessy as the latter listened to confessions from members of the flock. The Father did all the counselling and Banta was by his side, learning.

The voice sounded like a lady in her thirties. 'Forgive me, father, for I have sinned.'

'Tell me, what have you done?'

'I...I...have committed adultery,' came a faltering answer.

'How often?' asked the Father.

'Thrice.' It seemed easier once the secret was out.

'Repentance is the first step, my child. Say a prayer, put five dollars into the donation box, and stay on the right path. God bless you.'

The lady thanked the Father and left the booth. After a few more confessions of stealing, anger, etc. there was an overwrought young man.

'Father, I'm afraid I have sinned. I committed adultery, not once, not twice, but three times!'

The Father's voice was kind but strong. 'You are repentant, that is the right thing. Say a prayer, put five dollars into the donation box, and see that you do not commit the sin again. God bless you, my son.'

Banta was absorbing every word and nuance of the Father's techniques. So impressed was Father O'Shaughnessy with the assistant's diligence that he suggested Banta should handle the next confession while he (Father O'Shaughnessy) stepped out to return a phone call from the bishop.

'Father, I need your help. I have committed adultery.' The voice was of a young woman barely in her twenties.

'How many times, my child,' Banta asked softly. 'Oh, just one time,' answered the girl.

'Oye, you are in luck. We have a special going this week. Go and commit adultery two more times, repent, then come here, say a prayer and drop five dollars into the donation box, then don't do it again,' Banta replied cheerfully.

Commentary

Actually, at one time this very mode of absolution was in play in the highest realms of the Catholic Church. Pope Leo X would grant 'indulgences' to wealthy people, allowing them forgiveness for their sins in exchange for donations. There were even various rates for different kinds of indulgences. One of the main criticisms of Martin Luther against the Church was regarding this practice.

On a wider scale, the joke underscores the reality that organized religion has a powerful mercantile aspect, causing the temporal and the worldly to overshadow the spiritual and the ideal, even polluting everyday living. An article by columnist Aakar Patel brings this out beautifully with respect to India.[9]

---

[9]'Our gold-plated culture of corruption', *Livemint*, 28 April 2011; http://tinyurl.com/goldplated-culture-of-corrupt

Upon Reflection

Banta and his wife were sitting in an auto rickshaw on their way home after a romantic lunch at the mall. A couple of times during the ride, Banta thought he had caught the driver admiring his wife, stealing a glance at her image in the rear-view mirror. He ignored it.

Then he caught him glancing again, and decided he should say something.

'*Oye, najraan road te rakheen* (Hey, keep your eyes on the road),' he hissed, with a frown.

The driver mumbled, 'Hanji, sardarji (Yes, sardarji),' and kept driving. The droning hum of the auto and the effects of a heavy lunch, together, conspired to make Banta Singh nod off for a short while. The sound of a passing truck woke him up. Once again he found the fellow stealing a glimpse of the lady in the mirror.

'*Oye, gaddi rok hune* (Stop the vehicle immediately)!' he yelled at the driver. The edge in the voice did not leave any room for doubt. The auto rickshaw was soon pulled over on the side of the road.

Banta got out, and hauling the driver from his seat by the collar, he began to administer a series of Punjabi oaths interspersed with slaps. When he paused, the driver was cowering, wondering what else was in store. Banta meditated over a suitable solution. Finally he spoke.

'*Bahut ho giya sheeshe wichhon akkhaan ladauna* (Enough

of your dalliance through the mirror). *Hunn tu ^&%$^ pichhe baith, gaddi assaan chalawaange* (Now you ^&%$^ sit back, I'll do the driving)!'

Commentary

This sort of thinking has become so commonplace in the daily news as to not even attract notice anymore. Unable to tolerate the pinprick that was Saddam Hussain, America ended up sinking trillions of dollars into an immoral, illegal and worst, imbecilic, military adventure that eventually ended up delivering Iraq to a backseat where America's reputed adversary, Iran, sat waiting!

The Uncertainty Principal

Banta Singh dropped off his six-year-old son at school. After saying goodbye to the youngster, he made his way to the outside. It was as he neared his parked motorcycle when he remembered the letter he intended to give the teacher, to say his son would be absent for a few days next week as the family was going out of town to attend a wedding.

The class was in progress, and Banta did not wish to interrupt. He stood outside, unobtrusively, watching. The regular class teacher seemed to be away, and the principal was filling in. She was teaching addition.

'So, what is six plus two?' she said, nodding her head as she wrote, in big letters, '6 + 2 =' on the board. Several hands went up. She called on one of the kids, who answered, '8'.

'Very good,' the principal beamed, as she added '8' to what she had written before. On the next line she wrote, '5 + 3 = ?', and below that she wrote, '4 + 4 = ?'.

After waiting a minute, she turned and replaced both '?'s with '8'. She stepped back, looked at the board quizzically, then turned to the class without a change of expression, saying, 'Hmm...'

Banta could not take it anymore, and left very disturbed. That evening at dinner, he broke the news to his wife that they might have to find a new school for the son. It was not a trivial matter. He explained why.

'*Oye, lagda hai ki principal nu siddi-siddi ginnati vi ni aundi hai* (It doesn't look like even the principal is entirely certain about simple additions),' Banta said to his wife. 'For eight, sometimes she says six plus two, sometimes five plus three, sometimes four plus four. At this rate how can the children be sure of anything?'

Commentary

And this with the most concrete of all subjects—arithmetic! Wait till the child gets old enough to tackle humanities, where there are two, if not more, sides to every question. The urge for certitude seems an inescapable human frailty, the belief that there is only one right answer to every question, a far more destructive one, historically.

The effort to simplify is entirely valid, even noble, for it is what makes it possible for us to comprehend the world to the extent we can. Wisdom lies in knowing where to stop. As Einstein said, 'Everything should be made as simple as possible, but not simpler.'

Visualisingh

Banta Singh was interviewing at a leading security company, well-known for its services to top secret manufacturing units dealing with highly sensitive parts and rare materials. His interviewer was a qualified psychologist, wishing to gauge how potential candidates would respond to sudden and unexpected challenges.

'Okay, Banta. Now I'm going to ask you to shut your eyes and imagine this. Imagine you are making your rounds through the inner walkway of the plant one evening. Suddenly you hear a small explosion, and see a series of sparks coming from the cooling unit below. Imagine that the unit now catches fire. You know what bad things can happen if the cooling unit is compromised. Now imagine that you notice a couple of workers rush to the unit with fire extinguishers. Meanwhile, imagine that you hear gunshots and see one of the workers clutch at his shoulder and drop to the ground...

and imagine the chaos in the plant with people screaming in fear and running helter-skelter...'

'Tell me, Banta, what would you do in such a situation?'

'Oye, vary simpal,' Banta replied with a triumphant smile. 'I will just stop imagining.'

Commentary

Just as truth is vastly stranger than fiction, imaginary scenarios are severely limited compared to real ones. Not for nothing is the statement that all war plans go out the window the moment the first shot is fired.[10] Specific training allows individual components to work smoother, but it is impossible to provide 100 per cent protection against mishaps overall. For example, putting out the fire involves knowing where the extinguisher is and knowing how to use it. People can be trained to do this. Similarly, areas of safety and the quickest path to reach these areas may also be taught. All such training minimizes but does not eliminate dangers from unexpected sequencing of events.

The deeper import of Banta's reply is that the only solution to imaginary problems is to stop imagining them, a startlingly simple but powerful truth. In an age when a fair percentage of the population is receiving psychological

---

[10]'No battle plan ever survives contact with the enemy.' Attributed to Prussian Field Marshall Helmuth Karl Bernhard Graf von Moltke (1800-1891)

care and names like Prozac and Zoloft are part of our everyday vocabulary, Banta's approach seems exceptionally relevant.

A Breath-taking Discovery

Banta Singh listened with rapt attention as the teacher spoke. The chemistry lesson that day seemed to hold a great deal of meaning for him. His face was sombre and it was only with much difficulty that he maintained his composure during the rest of the day in school. That evening, he shared his emotional upheaval as he sat with his friend Santa Singh.

'*Oye, tainnu pataa hae* (Hey, do you know), just today I came to realize, oxygen was discovered by some French guy called Lavoisier only in 1777.'

'*Taan mainnu ki* (So, what do I care),' shrugged Santa, a commerce student who had stayed away from science with good reason.

'*Oye khottiya* (You ass), don't you understand? Oye, I thanked Waheguru (Almighty) that I was only born after 1777. If I were born before I shudder to think how I would have even survived!'

Commentary

On the face of it, Banta is being ridiculous; but he is pointing to a serious aspect of our thinking. Robert Pirsig says something close to this in his classic, *Zen and the Art of Motorcycle Maintenance*.

'The law of gravity and gravity itself did not exist before Isaac Newton...and what that means is that law of gravity exists nowhere except in people's heads! It's a ghost! Laws of nature are human inventions, like ghosts. Law of logic, of mathematics are also human inventions, like ghosts.'

Which is to say, our 'world' is itself a construction enjoined by the models (ghosts?) we use to define or study it. Many of our troubles arise because we become more attached to the model than the reality it is supposed to help represent.

Ab Buzz Karo, Bahut ho Gaya

Banta Singh was frustrated. It was 2 a.m. and although he had retired to bed by 10 o'clock last night, he had barely slept half an hour. The villain thwarting his repose was a lone but determined mosquito. Every time, just as he was dropping away to sweet sleep, it would commence flitting around the room buzzing, 'ooooooonnnn...', waking him up. He decided it was time to teach the little pest a lesson. He thought a good deal, and soon came up with a plan.

His own luck, and a moment of cocky insouciance on the part of the mosquito, soon combined to turn the tide in Banta's favour. A general swipe towards the sound of the buzz brought the mosquito in the custody of his right hand. It continued to buzz inside his closed fist for a few minutes, and then settled down quietly. It was exactly the opportunity for which Banta was waiting. He waited a little longer, in dead silence. Then, bringing his closed hand slowly towards his mouth, taking care not to disturb the mosquito, he gave a big smile before loudly going 'oooooooooooonnn' into his closed fist, and said, '*Hunn ^&%$^ patta lagya tainnu ke mainnu kivein lagda hai* (^&%$^, now do you understand how it feels to me)?'

Commentary

Once again Bernard Shaw's admonition regarding doing unto others as you would have them do unto you comes to mind, but in a reverse context. The punishments you dread too, might not be the same ones that give your enemies sleepless nights (no pun intended). There is no better illustration of this truth than the old Brer Rabbit story of the briar patch.[11]

---

[11]See a rendition here, http://tinyurl.com/2fssknu

Embarassingh

It was just Banta Singh's misfortune. This was the third time in the last couple of months that he had been hauled up in court; and each time before the same judge, a well-known curmudgeon. They were all minor offenses in Banta's mind. The first time it was because he had argued with a cop over where he had parked his motorcycle. The second time it had been an altercation with someone who had cut ahead of him in the line at the bank. Today he was in for a loud argument in front of a bar that had eventually led to a mild scuffle.

As he was reflecting on fate, there was a sudden hubbub in the courtroom; the judge was entering. Once he had settled down, the business of the day began; the first case was Banta's. The judge customarily wore an attitude of disgust. As soon as he saw Banta, his manner turned even more austere. Even worse, the judge had a fine memory.

Scowling as he glared at Banta, he said slowly, '*Oye puttar, eh teeji vaar aithhe tainnu vekh rihan. Eh koi sh'reefaan di jagah hai? Sharm ni aundi tainnu* (Son, this is the third time I am seeing you here. Is this any place for decent people? Have you no shame)?'

Banta could not contain himself.

'*Mu'af karna judge sahib, tussi khud vi tah aithhe roj roj aunde ho, tuhannu ni sharm aundi* (Forgive me judge sahib, you yourself come here every day, don't you feel any shame)?!'

Commentary

The trite answer would be that there is an essential difference between a habitual offender and a judge, who is daily in the courtroom. The deeper significance, both of the judge's remark and of Banta's flippant reply, lies in a universal reality: the environment seeps into the human soul. Many are the novels, even classics, which feature the slow descent of the fresh, idealistic, policeman, lawyer or journalist into a blasé, hard-boiled, cynical—even corrupt—accessory to the all-consuming black hole that is society's underbelly.

Ring Is King

A friend called out to Banta Singh one evening as he was out on his walk. Pulling over his motorbike close to where Banta stood on the sidewalk, the friend asked, 'Oye Bante, is there a problem with your phone?'

'No, it is working fine,' replied Banta, pulling out a brand-new smart phone from his pocket.

'Hmm...that's surprising. I've been trying to call you for a week. And all I get is a message that keeps repeating, "This number is currently switched off".'

Banta threw his head back and chuckled. 'Oye, hunn main samjhya (Oh, now I understand),' he smiled at his friend. 'That is my new caller tune!'

Commentary

Banta has illustrated one of the most significant problems in computer language, indeed, in language itself. This is the problem of delimiters. A delimiter is something which tells the reader of a change in context. The simplest example of a delimiter is the quotation mark. Whenever you come across it, you immediately treat the words that follow as different from the earlier text, all the way until you reach the close quotation mark. You can see why this might present some challenges. Even in the previous sentence, had I used, '"', instead of the word, 'quotation', you would have had to pause and think about what was meant. Now imagine the confusion if an article (or indeed, even an entire book) is all about the quotation mark. The author would have to use other kinds of delimiters to disambiguate between when the '"' sign is being used to signify a quote beginning or end, and when it is being used just as the character itself. Often, in computer programs, this is achieved by placing an 'escape' character in front of a sign so that the reader (typically, a computer program) would know that the sign was not to have a special significance. Then there is the other problem of escaping the 'escape' character! It can all get quite hairy and rather intricate to debug.

    The solution, in everyday life, is to use delimiters that are very, very, unlikely to be confused with the actual content. The absence of this precaution is at the centre of the Abbott and Costello classic, 'Who's on First'[12].

---

[12] Watch it here, https://www.youtube.com/watch?v=kTcRRaXV-fg

A Pole-ish Joke

The elderly passer-by was stopped in his tracks. He had been watching, transfixed, for the better part of an hour. The drama taking place in front of him had put pause to his usual morning walk. A group of sardars were engaged in trying to measure the height of a flag pole. One of them would shimmy up the pole carrying one end of a tape measure. It would slip, causing him to have to slide down in order to retrieve it. On the one or two occasions, he was able to successfully go as far as the tape stretched, another would need to bring the tape up so that he could go further up and measure the next length. Nearly an hour into this exercise, frustration was mounting and tempers were fraying.

The passer-by was an engineer by profession, and a kindly soul too. He approached the group slowly, and asked politely if he could venture a suggestion. This was welcomed all around.

'Perhaps, I was thinking...,' he began, 'you could lift the pole off the base...if you laid it flat on the ground, you could measure it easily. See what I mean?'

A round of shy smiles greeted this speech. No one wanted to be disrespectful to an elder. Finally, one member of the group found the right words to let the buzurg[13]

---

[13] Elder

down gently, 'Thank you for your idea, sirjee. But you see, we want the height of the pole, not the width.'

Commentary

The joke is an interesting example of how we may confuse the intrinsic characteristics of something with our external description of it. That there are three dimensions to a physical object is out of question. However, concepts such as length, breadth, depth, width, height, etc. depend on how we look at the object. Most of the time, we take into account the nature of the object in speaking of its width, height, etc. In the case of a flagpole, clearly the longest dimension would have to be the height. But this is not something that a pure measurement exercise would consider. (See also 'In Plane Sight' in *Bantaism*).

Making Thermos of It

Banta Singh was captivated by the sleek, shiny, tall, minaret-like new object that rested upon his colleague's desk. The instant the latter finally returned from his meeting, Banta asked him what it was.

'I'm tired of that concoction they're calling chai in the canteen downstairs,' said the colleague. 'I decided to bring my own from home hereafter. So I went and bought this thermos,' he explained.

It was a word that Banta had never heard before. 'But, won't the chai get cold,' he wondered.

'Ah you see, that's the beauty of a thermos,' the colleague began to wax eloquent. 'It keeps hot things hot for hours.' Then he added, remembering what he had read in the little manual, 'And also cold things cold.'

It was enough to convince Banta that he too needed this contraption. That same evening, he went to the department store where his colleague had purchased his thermos, and obtained a lovely looking replica of the other's maroon flask, but in teal blue. Next morning, the colleague found him sitting with a smile on his face. On

Banta's desk was his new thermos.

'Fast work! Nice colour, too,' the colleague complimented Banta. 'What have you got in it?'

Banta replied, beaming, 'One chai, one coffee, and one Coca-Cola.'

Commentary

Sometimes, our belief in technology surpasses itself. The colleague had said the flask would keep hot things hot and cold things cold. He did not add that this wasn't a simultaneous proposition.

Personalisingh

The bus grunted as it approached the stop. There was a scribble on a black signboard resting against the front window. It probably told of the bus's destination, but only if one could decipher it. No surprise, then, that the assembled passengers at the bus stop all made a rush to the door to ask whether the bus was going where they wanted to go.

By the time Banta had reached the bus, sprinting as he had been and almost out of breath, much of the sorting had already taken place. Those whose destination fell along the bus's route had clambered onto it, and those who had found out it wasn't headed their way were back in the shade of the bus stop. There was just one gentleman, who looked like a foreigner, at the door of the bus trying to ask the driver a question. 'Will this bus take me to Amritsar?' he asked in an accented English.

'No sir,' the driver replied politely. The foreigner said thank you and turned back towards the bus shelter.

Right behind the foreigner stood Amritsar-bound Banta Singh, who eagerly asked the driver, 'Will it take me?'

Commentary

Much has been written, including the famous essay by the late scholar A.K. Ramanujan[14], about the different meanings the same sentence can produce depending on where the emphasis is placed. The foreigner's was placed on 'Amritsar'. Whereas Banta sensed that it was on 'me'. The fact that the guy was a foreigner perhaps played some kind of a role, maybe the refusal by the driver had to do with the man's descent! This deafness to emphasis, if not to tone, is widely prevalent, save for the best communicators who, naturally, are also excellent listeners.

There is also the matter of usage. Rarely do Indians put themselves as part of the question in such inquiries. 'Does this bus go to XYZ?' is more the usual form. In

---

[14]'Is There an Indian Way of Thinking?' by A.K. Ramanujan, in *India Through Hindu Categories*, edited by McKim Marriott, 1990

the West, they often phrase this query exactly the way the foreigner did here. Whether this is because the Indian regards the bus system as merely an external agency which excludes any notion of personal investment, while the other considers the bus service and himself to be in a more symbiotic connection, may be a matter for some interesting speculation, with the bus system serving as a symbol for the world at large.

A Khali Dal[15]?

Banta Singh had just left the exam hall. He had stayed a bare 20 minutes to answer a three hour long test. Most of his time inside had been spent staring at the questions in an attitude of complete bemusement, shaking his head over and over. Finally, he had risen from his seat without ever putting pen to paper, turned in his empty answer sheet and left the hall.

He was looking out into the blue sky, still contemplating the enormity of having left a final exam blank, when he heard a voice whispering his name from behind. It was Santa Singh, his friend, philosopher and classmate, who had been sitting right next to him in the exam hall.

---

[15] An empty group

Before Banta could say anything, Santa said, 'Oye, ajj tah anneh kuttay hirnan de shikari wali gal ho gayi. Ik vi swaal palle ni piya. Main tah ^&%$^ paper khaali chhad aaya (Oye, it was a matter of blind dogs hunting the deer! Couldn't understand a single question. I just left the entire ^&%$^ paper blank).'

Banta was listening to his friend with a rising apprehension that showed on his face. He didn't think Santa fully understood the consequence of what he had just revealed. He was aghast. 'Oye, tainnu pataa vi hai tu ki kar aaya? Saanu dovaan nu hunn ^&%$^ college ton suspanded samajh (Oye, do you even know what you've ended up doing? Consider both of us suspended from the ^&%$^ college now).'

Santa looked at him in disbelief. 'Suspand kis waaste? Koi vaddi gal ni, paper ^&%$^ agle s'mayster'ch pher de diyaange (Suspend for what? It's no big deal, we just do the ^&%$^ paper over again next semester).'

Banta had a withering expression on his face. 'This is no longer an academic issue,' he explained. 'Oye bewaqoofa, I also left the paper blank. You know the penalty for plagiarism. When they see that both of us have turned in blank papers, they are going to think we've copied from each other!'

Commentary

During the Emergency rule of the late Prime Minister Indira Gandhi, a rigid press censorship was clamped on publications. In the first few days following its imposition, some newspaper editors sought to show their defiance of authoritarianism by leaving their editorials blank. They might not have had identical views, but certainly there was unanimity in their attitude to censorship, a surmise hardly likely to have escaped the censors. In this instance, Banta's conclusions are unfounded, but there is a grain of truth in his thinking. The authorities might well regard both these close pals turning in an empty answer sheet as indicative that the association is doing neither much good by way of studies!

The point is, while the data itself might not be significant in some instances, the metadata (data about the data) might very well be. This is at the heart of the controversy surrounding the Edward Snowden revelations regarding the unauthorized electronic snooping by the NSA.[16]

A Khali Gal[17]

Banta and Bachittar had decided to organize a private communication system based on carrier pigeons. Pretty

---

[16] An excellent discussion on data vs metadata is part of this debate, http://www.munkdebates.com/debates/state-surveillance. See also, Former CIA director: 'We kill people based on metadata', http://rt.com/usa/158460-cia-director-metadata-kill-people/

[17] An empty matter

soon, they had a fleet of birds organized, all superbly trained, efficient and accurate. Not for them the ubiquitous complaints about dead spots and network failures. A tiny scroll attached to a ring around a pigeon's neck guaranteed an excellent user experience, to say nothing of the pleasure in knowing that there would never be a call from desperate marketeers peddling their wares at all hours of day and night. Both of them agreed that this was vastly better than carrying around a cellphone.

Things were working beautifully when one day, a carrier pigeon landed near Bachittar. He picked up the pigeon and gently extracted the paper rolled up at its neck. He opened it out to read, only to find it was blank. There was nothing written on it. He could make no sense of this at all. Had someone intercepted the pigeon and replaced the scroll? All kinds of wild possibilities raced through his mind. Finally he decided it was best to resolve this face-to-face. He got in his car and drove straight to Banta's place 50 miles away, taking the pigeon and the little blank scroll with him.

After hearing his friend's worried account, Banta Singh smiled and said, '*Fikr di koi gal ni, kaka. Main sirf tainnu ik miss kaal de riha si* (Nothing to worry about. I was just giving you a missed call).'

Commentary

That the absence of information could itself be information is famously highlighted by the Sherlock Holmes story,

'Silver Blaze'. In more mundane terms, the expression, 'no news is good news' does the same. Banta's concept is quite a sound one. The fact that most people in India use the missed call as a way to communicate without incurring a toll, does not detract from the deeper aspect of this joke. The paper here might be blank, but that hardly makes it devoid of meaning!

Wall-to-wall Boasting

Banta Singh and his brother were trading arguments. As often happens in such situations, the exchange descended rapidly until they were soon at a level of insults, of showing each other down. Banta lost no time in rubbing in his accomplishments.

'*Mere kol alishaan bangla hai, Benj di gaddi hai, Chhattarpur'ch farmhouse hai, dollar da 'count hai, tameshare hai...tere kol ki hai, oye* (I've got a swanky bungalow, a Mercedes Benz, a farmhouse in Chhattarpur, a foreign bank account, a timeshare. What've you got, oye)?'

After all these years, his twenty-eight theatre viewings of *Deewar* as a young man were finally serving some practical purpose.

'*Te mer kol vi panthouse hai, comp'ny hai, BMW hai, orchard hai, yacht hai* (I too have a penthouse, my own company, a BMW, an orchard, a yacht),' responded the brother, who had seen the same movie almost as many times. In his mind he was going over other assets to list as he waited for Banta's reply.

But Banta was looking as if he had been kicked in the stomach. His face was clouded over with a sudden realization that had hit him like a thunderbolt. It was a few seconds before he could find the words to express his anguish, 'Oye ^&%$^, taa pher...ma kidde kol hai (Oh ^&%$^, then in that case...who's got the mother)?'

Commentary

The joke is based on one of the most celebrated exchanges in Indian cinema, from the film, Deewar, meaning 'wall'. A single mother has two sons. The elder joins a criminal gang; the younger the police force. The gangster son becomes rich and opulent, while his brother has just his lowly police salary. When the elder brother throws at his sibling's face all the impressive possessions he has amassed, taunting him to name anything he may have that could even remotely compare, the younger brother, in a line which has passed into history, demolishes him with the words, 'I have Mother'.

Mother, in the film, the epitome of sacrifice representing all that is good and noble in the world before whose shining glory all the glitter of worldly goods appears dull, resides only where honesty and uprightness are found, even if this means a life of poverty instead of wealth.

The joke is a window on a social ethos that has come a long way since the making of *Deewar*, a milieu where acquisition has become a universal, and sole, precept and a glimpse at the cost.

Of Words and Forwards

Even though he had been walking on air ever since he had got the news of his daughter's birth earlier that morning, Banta Singh wasn't so completely lost in joy as to miss a certain coldness in his father-in-law's latest, 'Hello'. Banta had been calling him every half hour to check up on how his wife and baby were doing. As far as Banta could recall, the old man had been perfectly cordial as late as the previous time they spoke. He decided to confront the matter directly by calling and asking, 'Everything okay? Anything wrong?'

'Yes, something is wrong. No, no, mother and baby are fine. But your wife is pretty angry with you. And so are all of us,' his father-in-law replied. Then the line went dead. The old man had snapped his ancient clamshell phone shut!

This wasn't a case of 'pretty angry'; it seemed more like one of 'hopping mad'. Banta couldn't imagine what he could have done wrong, sitting in Delhi hundreds of miles away, to make his wife and her folks in Mumbai so upset. He tried to go over what he had done since the last conversation. Well, he had gone over to the halwai shop and purchased two large boxes of laddu to distribute to his colleagues. He had accepted all their felicitations before settling back in his chair and sending out an SMS of the news to all the contacts on his cellphone. What could be blameworthy in any of this, he was at a loss to fathom.

And if at all, he said to himself, there was anything wrong with the SMS, it was his father-in-law who was to blame. He had merely forwarded the message from the old man! He shook his head, and re-examined for the umpteenth time the perfectly innocuous SMS from his father-in-law, which read:

'Jeeto just delivered a beautiful baby girl.

Congratulations, u r now a proud father!'

Commentary

A perfect example of how the same content can have an entirely different construction in different contexts. Quibblers will carp that SMS forwards do include the original sender and receiver (simple answer: Banta pared down the message). As important as the context are the potential constructions and uses to which a communication may be put. Most of us have been in situations where we have found ourselves protesting: 'But that's not what I meant'. Part of good communication is visualizing how the recipient will view the message, and making sure there is no other, particularly mischievous, construction that may be placed on the message. Professionals spend a lot of time obsessing over potential word associations, puns, possibilities of misunderstanding or misquoting and the like. Communication is hard business, even though everybody who can speak or write a few grammatical sentences thinks he has mastered the art.

Against the Odds

The judge said he was happy to grant a divorce if the couple were able to reach an amicable settlement regarding their three young children. Herein lay the difficulty. For both Banta and his wife were sticklers for equality; every piece of common property was being divided exactly in half. The judge's condition therefore presented a seemingly insurmountable impasse. With an odd number of children, it was impossible that an equal number could stay with both father and mother.

After several days of consideration, Banta approached the judge again. His wife was also invited to be present. 'Your Lordship,' he began, 'I think I may have discovered a fair resolution.'

The judge was entirely curious what this might be. He leaned forward eagerly.

'I think we should have another child,' Banta continued, with a glance at his wife. 'We can put off the divorce until next year, when we should be able to divide up the children fairly!'

Commentary

There is an old saying, 'things have to get worse before they can get better'. A little thought will reveal a whole variety of situations where the saying holds true. For example, there are insurance policies that will not cover a minor illness but only major ones. Once the cold degenerates into pneumonia is when the patient may expect help. The other saying, 'the darkest hour is before dawn', also illustrates the same idea. One of the chief impediments to solving the Rubik's Cube is the unwillingness to break up a face which has been made uniform in colour. To reach the full solution, sometimes one must be willing to give up partial perfections.

Thus Spake Banta Singh

A blind Parsi walks into a bar. Finding his way to the counter, he seats himself carefully upon a bar stool, smiles at the bartender and then orders a large beer.

'First drink is always on the house for new guests,' says the bartender cordially, as he plunks a tall beer mug in front of this unfamiliar customer.

'Thank you,' responds the Parsi, taking a good gulp. 'Aaah, just the thing I needed. Now, who would like to hear an insanely funny sardar joke?' he beams, turning his head from left to right.

'Before you do that, Bawa,' comes a deep voice sitting next to him on the right, 'let me give you a little guided tour of the situation here. The bartender is a sardar. The guy sitting to your left is a 6-foot three-time champion wrestler, and he's a sardar. The guy standing behind you is an ex-army major, a sardar. I am myself a sardar, always ready for a brawl, and the guy on my right is also a sardar, with a hair-trigger temper.'

'Now…think carefully. Do you still want to tell that sardar joke?'

The Parsi's face turns grim. He tosses back the last of the beer and motions to the bartender for another. Then he smiles and shakes his head, saying, 'Oh, na, na. I don't think so. Arre baba, who wants to be bothered explaining it five times?'

Commentary

'Love is blind' is received wisdom. It appears that courage is equally so. At least, appreciation of courage is. History is full of episodes where the adversary's courage succeeds in winning him respect and admiration. The English in India were chastened by the two Anglo-Sikh wars of the 19th century. Victorious though they were, their appreciation for the valour shown by the Sikhs was sky high. The Sikhs too gained huge respect for the small band of men fighting thousands of miles away from their home. This mutual esteem, arising from some of the fiercest battles, was to have great consequences for the course of Indian history in future decades. The same with the English wars with the Gorkhas.

The story is told of another Punjabi from long ago, Porus, a local king who fought bravely against Alexander. Brought up in chains to the Greek's presence after the battle, Porus conducted himself with such courage and dignity that a deeply impressed Alexander restored his kingdom to him.

In this current story, the Parsi would appear to have garnered respect from the others in the bar for his aplomb, perhaps to go home with more sardar jokes than he came in knowing!

Aquaphobia or Aap ko Kho Dia[18]?

Banta Singh was really getting worried about his wife. He had not yet worked up the gumption to speak with her directly, considering this had all the hallmarks of a psychological problem.

But he had to open his heart to someone. 'O'yaar, that too she used to be a champion long-distance swimmer,' he lamented to his friend Santa Singh. 'And now, suddenly, she is afraid of this tiny little bit of water? Oye, I tell you, this is the third time I've seen the life guard sitting in the bathtub with her!'

Commentary

As to the infinite human capacity for self-deception via comforting falsehoods, it is hard to improve on Ghalib:

> *Hum ko maaloom hai jannat ki haqeeqat lekin*
> *Dil ke khush rakhney ko Ghalib ye khayaal achhaa hai.*

(Translation)
We too know the truth about heaven but
To keep the heart happy, Ghalib, this idea is good.

---

[18] I lost thee

The Loonacy[19] of It All

An out-of-town customer, who had stopped by Banta Singh's small kirana store[20] to buy a box of matches, couldn't help but ask. He had noticed that 50 per cent of the space in the hole-in-the-wall shop was comprised of cartons of table salt. Salt appeared to be the predominant stock-in-trade of Banta's business.

'Arre sardarji, I wouldn't have imagined such heavy demand for salt in this small town. Thought people were cutting down on salt for health reasons. Looks like you must be selling hundreds of cartons of salt each month!'

'*Babuji, tuhannu sach gal dassaan* (Sir, to tell you the truth), I sell not more than 10 or 15 packets a month. You see, I'm not a very good salt seller,' Banta replied.

The customer was a little puzzled. 'Good salt seller? What's that?' he asked.

'Oh, yes,' Banta answered. 'There are good ones and there are bad ones. If you want to see a good one, you should meet the fellow who sells salt to me! Now, he is outstanding.'

---

[19] 'Loon' meaning 'salt' in Punjabi
[20] Grocery store

Commentary

A brilliant metaphor for the modern consumer. The 'good salt sellers' in our lives are the gigantic sales and advertising machines, which daily contrive to foist on us things we don't need and often don't use, and besides, make us feel good about it. The comedian George Carlin had an iconic act about the American mania for shopping.[21] In the last few decades, this disease has spread worldwide. We buy and buy, shutting our eyes to the fact that it is bye-bye both to our contentment and to the state of the environment. The joke also shows that there is nothing inevitable about our getting duped in this manner; we can stop it at any time by simply examining our real needs and realizing

---

[21]'George Carlin on America and Shopping Malls', http://www.youtube.com/watch?v=dSDU8Laoi2U

the stupidity of the endless consumption that ends up consuming us. Non-cooperation, in a nutshell.

Menu Ki?

Banta Singh had been on hold for a good half an hour now. He had called tech support because his new computer was freezing up. He was a complete novice and this was his first call to get some help. He could barely contain his impatience as he was transferred back and forth before being placed in a limbo where he listened to filler music, his neck tilted sideways to hold the cordless phone in place while he made himself some tea in the kitchen. He had just finished pouring out a cup and was stirring in the sugar when a human voice came on the line.

'Hi, this is BK from technical support. How can I help you?'

Several more minutes after giving his name, where he had bought the computer, etc., Banta Singh finally got a chance to explain the problem. The tech listened patiently, asking a few questions along the way, and then said, 'No problem, Mr Singh. Are you at your computer right now, sir?'

Banta replied that he was not.

'Please go to your computer, Mr Singh. Tell me after it is switched on. I will hold, sir, no problem.' Banta did as suggested. In a little while the computer was all fired up. 'Yes, I'm at the computer and it is switched on,' he reported to the tech.

'Yes, sir. That's great, sir. Now, sir, if you would please go to "My Computer..."'

The tech could not complete his sentence, for he was buried under an avalanche of Punjabi gaalis from the other end. Banta was already in a sullen mood, exhausted by the long wait. And now this young smarty-pants seemed to be playing the fool with him.

'Oye do you think I am bewaqoof? First you make me go to my computer. And when I get there you want me to ^&%$^ go all the way to *your* computer? I don't even ^&%$^ know where you are!'

Commentary

Banta Singh, computer neophyte, could not possibly have imagined that his computer had a menu item called 'My Computer'. Naturally he presumed the tech was using the phrase to refer to his own computer! It underscores the fact that, although the worlds of the computer literate and the computer illiterate are quite disparate, the words employed in the two are frequently the same, yet different in connotation and meaning. Think of words like menu, mouse, window, icon, memory and the like.

'Cat Burglar' – a Whole New Meaning

A sardar was in London attending a one week course for top-notch burglars. Naturally, neither the existence of such an academy nor its location was known other than to a select community of burglars at the head of their craft. The gentleman teaching this course was a small, mild-mannered, soft-spoken individual. Known in underworld circles as 'Ernie the elf', he had been the toast of skilled burglars everywhere before he had dropped word of his retirement a few years before. When the idea of setting up an elite burglary institute was mooted, Ernie's was one of the first names to pop up as a potential faculty member. And as honours go, the sardar too was among only five professionals on three continents to be admitted to this inaugural 'by invitation only' course. It had been a tough and demanding week, he thought to himself, but how much he had learnt from this great man!

'Now, lads, you are all bloody tops, and don't you let anybody tell you otherwise, will you?' said Ernie in his final lecture. 'But remember this, things can go south any time, right? What you always want to do is have a Plan B.' He went on to tell them a story about a time when the house owner, who slept with a revolver under the pillow, had been woken up by the noise of a floorboard creaking when Ernie was ransacking his room. Thinking quickly,

Ernie had meowed like a cat. Fortunately, it had worked. The man had been lulled and gone back to sleep.

Back in Amritsar the following month: the sardar lost no time in planning a burglary on a mansion belonging to one of the leading plutocrats in the city, Sardar Banta Singh. Thus did he and a couple of associates find themselves in Banta's bedroom at 3 a.m. in the morning. Banta was fast asleep. His wife was out of town. The burglars were working on the safe in the far corner of the gigantic sleeping quarters. A low, long, creak announced the success of their efforts, as the safe door slowly swung wide open. Nothing loud, but the noise had disturbed Banta. The snoring stopped abruptly, and came a voice, drowsy, not yet quite awake, 'Oye ^&%$^, *kaun hai oye* (Hey, who the ^&%$^ is that)?'

With a finger to his lips, the sardar motioned to his associates to keep calm. He had the matter well in hand;

thanks to Ernie, he had practised over and over against this very eventuality.

'*Ji main billi haan* (Sir, I'm a cat),' he twanged, in a credible imitation of a talking cat.

The next few seconds seemed an eternity.

'*Changa, changa… Main sochya kidre koi* ^&%$^ *chor-shor hove* (That's great. I was afraid it might be some ^&%$^ burglars or something),' came a languid reply before a steady snore resumed.

Commentary

It is the peril of every communication that the dross may register and the essence miss. In this instance it could not be said that the essence was lost. Instead, it was digested and improvised upon to what one would normally suppose was an unsustainable degree. Yet, the joke also shows the force of Napoleon's wish, 'Give me lucky generals.' Who could have imagined that an act of rank imbecility would meet its match in such stunning fashion? Still, it is in fact much the truth. If we were caught and punished for every infraction, few of us would be left holding our heads high. Life is generally forgiving. Only we tend to forget this generosity when placed in a position to judge others.

Vish'ing[22] the Man-eater Goodbye

This is from the days of the hunter and naturalist Jim Corbett[23], in the first few decades of the 20th century. In one set of villages of the Kumaon region, the appearance of a man-eating tiger had caused considerable panic and disruption. Men and women were no longer free to go about their daily activities; every rustle of the bush, every squawk of the bird, every whistle of the wind, seemed to presage a tiger around the corner. Naturally, the famous colonel was soon invited to deal with the menace. Corbett followed his usual routine—tracking the spoor, setting up a water buffalo under a tree for bait, waiting patiently up on a machan[24] all night, the works. It all came to nothing. Tension in the area was now at quite a pitch. News of the great man himself coming a cropper day after day, night after night, was not one to induce cheer.

It was at this point that one Banta Singh was heard voicing some disparagement over the sahib's strategy and technique. I would have killed the man-eater in one day, he declared. Normally, he would have been ignored or

---

[22] 'Vish' meaning 'poison' in Punjabi
[23] Edward James 'Jim' Corbett (born: 25 July 1875 in Nainital, India, died: 19 April 1955 in Nyeri, Kenya) was a legendary British hunter and tracker-turned conservationist, author and naturalist, famous for hunting a large number of man-eating tigers and leopards in India
[24] A platform up on a tree branch from which hunters can watch/shoot game

laughed out of countenance, but matters were looking so bleak (nearly a dozen killings or maimings so far) that the people were desperate. The crowd suddenly regarded him with something approaching reverence. One elder opened his mouth to ask something, but Banta was speaking.

'*Oye, kamaal hai, aiddar tussi man-eater nu ^&%$^ p'hains khuwa rahe ho. Unne aana thodi na hai* (Oye, this is remarkable! Here you are offering a ^&%$^ water buffalo to a man-eater. Why would he even show up)?' he tossed his head to the side in disdain. 'I would do it very differently.'

The confidence with which these words were spoken had an electrifying effect on the audience. Immediately everyone wanted to know all the details of his idea.

'I will first need a sheeshi[25] of strong poison,' he began. 'I will go to where the tracks lead, and then sit down and drink the entire bottle. When the ^&%$^ man-eater da puttar[26] eats me, *ohddi gal khatam* (his story is over)!'

Commentary

Banta's formula is farcical, of course. But it helps illustrate a significant attitude to the world, one that continues to play a major role in our daily discourse over a century after this fictitious Jim Corbett setting. At issue is the celebration of life versus the celebration of death. This death wish is central to individual psychology, but it can

---

[25] A glass bottle
[26] Son of a man-eater

also pervade a cult, and sometimes even an entire culture.

Aakar Patel, in his writings, frequently alludes to the difference between 'honour' cultures versus others, where commerce (and therefore, compromise and conciliation) is of greater influence. The former mentality is frequently found among the youth (one reason why gangs seem to have such allure). An excellent example is to be found in these words from Huckleberry Finn, 'Tom told me what his plan was, and I see in a minute it was worth fifteen of mine for style...and maybe get us all killed besides.'[27]

The attraction of getting killed even when there is no compelling reason to sacrifice one's life is puzzling but wholly real. Even countries may not be exempt from this impulse—in columnist Irfan Husain's observation, 'Years ago, a western diplomat wrote that Pakistan was the only country in the world that negotiates with a gun to its own head.'

No Fan of Logic

It was dark in the house, hot and muggy. It was the peak of summer, and the power company had picked Banta Singh's locality for a four-hour power-cut each evening.

---

[27]*The Adventures of Huckleberry Finn* (Tom Sawyer's Comrade) by Mark Twain, 1884

A solitary candle on a saucer placed atop the centre table provided some faint lighting. But it was enough to illuminate Banta, sitting in his shorts and banyaan[28], and his fuming visage. He had every reason to be discombobulated. The rising heat from the earth was at its most vicious at this hour. He expostulated to his wife, '*Oye, pakha tah chala dendi* (At least you could turn on the fan).'

In the dim but steady flame of the candle, one could also catch the look of disdain that appeared on Jeeto's face. '*Pher karti na ohi sardaraan waali gal* (Again you are talking nonsense),' she shook her head and replied, '*je pakha chalawaan taa candal bujh ni jaoo* (if I turn on the fan, won't it blow out the candle)?'

---

[28] A singlet, usually worn as an undershirt

Commentary

It is an example of how statements that are perfectly true in isolation are rendered absurd by the surrounding context. If one could turn on the fan, it meant there was electricity and therefore, no need for the candle. (In India, candles are used mostly for utilitarian purposes, not for romantic ambience!)

Coming to One's Census

'Who was that?' Jeeto asked, as she saw Banta slam the front door. 'Some fellow saying something about some census-vensus. *Pataa ni ^&%$^ kithhon nikal ke aa jaande ne sadda tame barbaad karan vaaste* (Don't know from where they emerge to waste our time),' he fumed.

'*^&%$^ kainda hai, sardarji, desh di abaadi da pataa karaana hai* (The ^&%$^ says to me, sardarji, we want to find out the population of the country). *Main bewaqoof nu kiha, mainnu ki pataa desh di abaadi ki hai, jihnnu pataa hove ohnnu ja puchh* (I told the fool, how the hell should I know the country's population, go ask someone who knows).'

Commentary

A nice illustration of the particle and the aggregate. We

tend to treat macro concepts and statistics as if they stood on their own, forgetting that they are merely collations of many small, often miniscule pieces of data, matter, etc. A notional macro concept or figure frequently takes on a life of its own, acquiring a status that eludes its more real (and living) components—human beings, animals, trees, etc.

Paint IT!

Dr Jain was a world-renowned management consultant. He had made his name by publishing several path-breaking research papers on efficiency. Especially, his forte was innovative techniques, to take advantage of information technology to avoid repetitive tasks. His services were in great demand among the Fortune 100 companies, he was on the board of directors of several well-known firms and an adviser to many international organizations and national governments. He was also a wealthy man owning several palatial homes on several continents, and more to the point of our story, was currently looking for somebody to paint the interior of one of his homes.

Santa Singh and Banta Singh were unemployed young men looking to earn some money. Not particularly skilled at anything, it seemed like a godsend to them when a friend pointed to an advertisement seeking painters for a seven bedroom luxury apartment in a swank high-rise in the city. House painting was something with which they did have some experience, having worked part-time at a construction company the previous year.

They were surprised to see Dr Jain at the apartment. As students in college, they had attended a special lecture by him. After showing them around the place, he asked how long they would take to do the job. He wanted it to be finished in five days, but all the house painters he had spoken to so far, wanted two weeks. His Efficiency could simply not understand why things had to be so tardy in India. Banta winked at Santa, and said, 'Oye sirjee, we can finish it in three days.'

Dr Jain was delighted. He gave them detailed instructions regarding colours, where to purchase supplies, etc., a 30 per cent advance payment, and told them he would be back in three days.

True to their word, Santa and Banta finished right on schedule. They called Dr Jain and told him he could inspect the apartment at his convenience. The efficiency expert had not really expected them to finish so quickly. He had just said five days to put some pressure. This was amazing, he told himself as he stepped out of his car and walked towards the elevator. These two fellows were better than his best students if they were this efficient, he said to himself.

He inspected the apartment with rising anger, but somehow couldn't stifle a feeling of having been outclassed at his own game.

In every room, only the ceiling had been painted, but perfectly. On each wall there were letters painted in excellent and tasteful calligraphy, 'Same as above'!

Commentary

Information can be shared, but not everything, even in this increasingly data-driven world of ours, is information. How nice it would be to take care of dinner by reading the words, 'same as yesterday's'. Still, there are many realms, aesthetics included, where we attempt to satisfy a mental or emotional need, not a physical one. If Banta, and Santa's technique were in fact showcased by our efficiency meister here, it could very well become the rage. Many new fashions actually begin in this manner.

An Accident of History

Banta Singh and his friend, Bachittar, both truck operators from Punjab, were visiting a travelling exhibit featuring artefacts from the Egyptian Museum. They were generally unimpressed by the collection, but paused a long while in front of one particular exhibit. It was the mummy of a new kingdom pharaoh. Swathed in heavy bandages and showing a dented skull, they found this one fascinating.

After musing for some time, Banta whispered to his friend, '*Oye, eh banda vichaara j'roor koi laari de accidant'ch mariya hona hai* (This poor guy certainly must've lost his life in a lorry accident).'

After examining the mummy from all sides, even Bachittar, generally disposed to argue with anything Banta said, was compelled to agree. '*Oye Bante, tu bilkul theek aakhya oye! Teh eh vi vekh* (Hey Banta, you are absolutely correct! And look at this too),' he said excitedly, dragging Banta to the other side of the mummy where there was a signboard, '1385 BC–1364 BC'. '*Jediyan do laariyaan da takkar hoya ohnaa de number vi ditte hoye ne* (And the two trucks which collided, they've even provided their license plate numbers)!'

Commentary

It is natural that we view everything in the light of our own background and experience. The absurdity of such a perspective is obvious enough when we look at others, but is as inescapable in our own daily perceptions and actions. As the old saying goes, 'To a man holding a hammer, everything looks like a nail'. It is equally easy to slip into a comfortable interpretation where we have to do the least work, not to disturb familiar patterns of thought, learn new facts, contend with competing hypotheses, etc.

Pran Jaaye Bin Button Dabaaye

It was one of the riskiest missions ever that he had undertaken. It was also to be his last; he knew that going in. But if he did succeed, it would be a blow from which the enemy would not lightly recover. For, Banta Singh had infiltrated the enemy's field command, a highly strategic and valuable hub of armaments, soldiery and logistics. His mission—a kamikaze attempt that would throw the enemy into total and utter disorder. He was strapped to the teeth with hidden explosives, enough to blow everything within a wide radius to smithereens with the press of a tiny button. It was all set. A last-minute scrambled communication to his headquarters for final clearance was all that was left before he committed suicide in the greater cause. He spoke into his tiny lapel mic, whispering, 'Sky is clear and stars are visible,' which was code for 'everything is set, ready to die'.

'Sirius will shine forever,' crackled the reply from high command, which meant, 'glory forever to you for your brave life, go ahead.' Banta muttered a silent prayer, then pulling out a dagger, plunged it into his stomach.

Commentary

Banta was so caught up in the suicide aspect of his mission that he forgot the bombing component. This of course is the joke here.

Could it be instead that he had decided at the last minute against sowing mayhem?

If the latter, he was certainly in good company. Arjuna had asked the same question before the start of the war in Mahabharata. Only Arjuna had asked Krishna, instead of putting the question silently to himself. It required 18 chapters of close convincing to shift Arjuna into first-gear for slaughter. There is a natural reticence and reluctance in human beings against doing harm to others. But once this is overcome, brainwashed by messages from society and conventional wisdom from 'elders', the same human being transforms into a willing and efficient instrument of destruction.

Say, Mr System

'*Oye, main kiha Bante, munde da janamdin ainni jaldi pher aagya? Mere khyaal chheh'k m'heene pehle ni manaaya si* (I say, Banta, your son's birthday has come around so quickly? If I remember, it was barely about six months ago that you celebrated it)?' his friend Bachittar asked, when Banta Singh gave him the invitation card for his son's upcoming birthday party.

'*Oye, bande nu tame de naal chalna painda hai. Tainnu ni pataa, ajj kal sab jagah s'maister system hi challan lagga hai* (Hey, one has to move with the times. Don't you know, these days it is all semester system everywhere),' Banta replied, giving his friend a pitying smile.

Commentary

Who wants to be seen as out of step with the times? The joke merely uses an exaggeration to highlight a general human frailty, the inability to resist peer pressure. The entire fashion industry is dependent on the belief that large numbers of people can be suckered into throwing away perfectly serviceable items of attire which were so 'must-have' only the previous year, and line up to buy new clothes whose fate too is akin to that of Shahryar's pre-Scheherazade wives.

A Patiala Pledge

A sardarji walked angrily back into a bar, in an unfamiliar neighbourhood in London, which he had just left after having a quick drink. Banging his fist hard on the counter, he demanded to be heard. A hushed silence fell on the assembly. Then he spoke, slowly, a hint of menace riding upon each syllable.

'I just went out and found my motorbike missing. Now, I'm going to say this just one time. If you know anything about it, make sure it is put back in place before I finish my next drink. Otherwise I swear I will do here what I did when this happened to me in Patiala. It is not pleasant, but I will be forced to do again what I did in Patiala. Please consider my words carefully.' He then settled down at the bar and ordered a scotch on the rocks, seemingly unaware of the hubbub he had caused around the pub.

After taking his time enjoying the drink, he paid and went outside, only to return in a minute. 'I appreciate your cooperation. Thank you all very much,' he boomed and then turned and left the bar.

The bartender, who had been aware of this kind of prank by some of the more boisterous elements among the clientele, was flabbergasted. This was the first time an item was ever restored so quickly and without a whole lot of negotiation and persuasion. His admiration for the sardar was matched only by his curiosity. He ran out to the parking lot just as the sardar was kick-starting his motorbike. 'Mr Singh, Mr Singh,' he yelled out from behind. The sardar turned around and gave him a pleasant smile. 'Mr Singh, just tell me, what exactly was that unpleasant thing you had to do in Patiala?'

A sad look came over the sardar's face. 'Oh, I had to forget about the motorbike and walk all the way home,' he replied.

Commentary

There are two aspects of interest here. One is straight from the poker player's manual: projecting strength even (particularly?) when one is dealt a weak hand. It is not how strong you are, it is how strong others think you to be. Many houses have a 'Beware of dog' sign outside. Only the most determined thief wants to investigate the truth of this claim.

The second element is that of preserving the mystique. The threat, as most parents invariably find out, is a lot more potent than actual punishment. It is in the interest of any negotiator to hint at a consequence rather than reveal all the details.

Car pe Farj[29] or Carpe Furs[30]?

A manhunt was underway. The local police force had been alerted to look for a known criminal suspected of a daring automobile robbery. The officer in-charge was giving a briefing to his subordinates on the fugitive. One of the slides he showed was a mug shot from the police files. Constable Banta Singh's hand went up. 'Sirjee, who took that picture?' he asked innocently.

'As a matter of fact, I did,' the officer replied with a wry smile. 'I had caught him in connection with a case five years back,' he recalled with a trace of pride. Banta Singh just could not understand this.

'*Sirjee, main samjhya ni. Jaddon saala hathh'ch phassya taan ohnu chhadd'ta. Hunn pher labh rahe ho* (Sir, I'm not sure I understand. When you had the bugger in your hands, you let him go. Now you are looking for him again)?'

Commentary

The officer probably explained to Banta that the man had served his time and could not be kept indefinitely, or that people could be arrested only for crimes they had committed, not for ones they were going to commit. However, Banta's

---

[29]Duty regarding the car
[30]Seize the thief (Latin)

question is being repeated by an increasing number of people in many parts of the civilized world. In some states of the USA, Banta's wish, in fact, has been written into the law. Called 'Three Strikes and You're Out', it means, a third offense is tantamount to a lifetime in jail (even if it is not serious enough to merit life-imprisonment). Owing to this law and other laws reflecting this attitude, the United States now has an astounding number of prisoners in jail per capita of the population, something like 1 or 2 per cent. It has been remarked that the United States has more people in prison not just per capita but in absolute numbers as compared to China, whose population is four times as large!

With life becoming hectic and stressful, populations in general are less spacious in their thinking and reasoning. The demand for instant solutions translates often into legislation that is short sighted and counter-productive. The death penalty is demanded for every variety of crime. The point that deterring crime is only one aspect of society's concerns is frequently lost in the din. Adding to all of this is the enthusiasm for privatizing large portions of the criminal justice system. Jailing large numbers of people then becomes an essential part of someone's bottom line. The consequences for life in general are frightening if this trend continues.

Habeas Corpus!

Santa and Banta, both bodybuilding enthusiasts, were poring over an online catalogue advertising the latest in physical fitness machines. They spent several hours discussing the relative merits of the various products, before telling each other they would think over what was best for each.

Banta was a fast decision maker. '*Oye, ajj di post'ch meri axercise machine pohnch g'yi* (Hey, my exercise machine was delivered by mail today),' Banta Singh reported to Santa excitedly over the phone a few days later. After a pause, he added, '*Mere khyaal ik-do din'ch kudi vi labh jaayegi* (I think, in a day or two I should be getting the girl too)!'

Commentary

Obviously Banta was under the impression that everything shown in the picture was part of the shipment! The joke is only an absurd exaggeration of a very real trick practically relied upon every day by advertisers. It is based on a notion in psychology that once a certain piece of information gets lodged in one's mind, it is very difficult to ignore, and biases the person's subsequent decisions even though it is of no relevance at all. This is why a furniture store shows you a beautiful sitting, dining or bedroom, complete with all the accessories. You might step in just to buy one item, but its impact on you when shown in a tasteful setting is a hundredfold more favourable than were you to see it in isolation. The use of good-looking men and women in ads serves to enhance the product—anchor their pleasing aspects in your mind—so that it is impossible for you to mentally separate the product from the model. Banta Singh has merely carried this from the subconscious into the openly stated.

Not Just a Face Lift

Banta Singh, his wife and teenage son were making their first visit to the big city. While Jeeto was admiring the flowers outside, Banta and his son decided to explore the lobby of a forty-story skyscraper. The youngster was totally excited by the atrium, and went off by himself, while Banta stood looking around. Suddenly, a couple of doors slid open in the wall in front of him. Two elderly ladies brushed past him to enter the small room. The doors slid shut. Banta watched in amazement. Five minutes later, the doors slid open again. A couple of beautiful young ladies emerged from within and hurried out to his left, leaving him engulfed in a whiff of perfume. Banta's jaw dropped. The doors slid shut. Three old ladies, one of them with a walking stick and another using a walker, slowly made their way around him to press a button on the wall. The doors opened again to admit them, then shut once more. A few minutes later, the doors opened, and would you believe it, three women in their twenties, their physical attributes manifest to all but the blind, stepped out.

Banta Singh waited no longer. Spotting his son admiring a life-size aeroplane model at the far end of the hall, he yelled out, '*Oye puttaraa, jarra baahron jaldi apni maa nu bulaa lai aayin* (Hey, son, quickly go fetch your mom from outside).'

Commentary

Science fiction giant Arthur C. Clarke wrote that any sufficiently advanced technology was indistinguishable from magic. Never having seen an elevator before, Banta concluded that it was a device for turning age into youth. There remains an interesting question, however. Why did he not think of entering this 'youth-giving' apparatus himself, instead of seeking to send his wife? It harks back to a natural blind spot common to all human beings, namely, to think that it is perfectly natural for everyone around us to age, while we ourselves remain the way we always were.

A Saal's Pitch[31]

Banta and the girl next door were now in an advanced state of courtship. But her family was extremely orthodox. There was no way they would accept a marriage where the groom was younger than the bride, she sobbed as she told Banta. There was no getting around the fact that Banta was born a year after the girl. When she had begun by saying there was an insurmountable problem, he had wondered what it could be. Now that she had told him, at their favourite meeting place—under the sisal tree close to the river—he could only smile at how upset the fairer sex became at the smallest problems. He first gave her his handkerchief and asked her to dry her eyes. Then he spent a few minutes telling her how beautiful she was and how much they were going to enjoy their lives together. She smiled for the first time that day. Suddenly, after a few minutes, she started crying again.

'But, but, you are still a year younger than me,' she protested through her tears. He figured it was time to play the trump card.

'*Oye, tu fiqr na kar soniye. Koi vaddi gal ni* (Don't you worry, O' Golden One. It's no big deal). Next year I'll be the same age as you. We'll just wait and get married next year!'

---

[31]'Saal' meaning 'year' in Hindustani and Punjabi

Commentary

The immediate absurdity aside, Banta's larger point regarding 'time' is worth some attention. Many things that seem supremely vital at the moment often turn out to be the proverbial 'much ado about nothing' in the long run. In twenty years time, will it really matter that Banta is a year younger than his wife? The relative significance of time itself changes over time. The difference between a one-year-old and a two-year-old is enormous; that between someone who is 39 and another who is 40 hardly significant. The Hindustani proverb, *unnees-bees ka farq* (the difference between 19 and 20, meaning, practically none)' underscores this very idea in terms of numbers.

Tall Tales

Three sardars were visiting Dubai, and had checked into a hotel located inside a skyscraper. They had been given a room on the 100th floor. When they left for dinner in the evening, the desk clerk called them over to let them know that they should return by midnight, because there was a scheduled power outage from 12 a.m. to 5 a.m. and the elevators would be down.

As it happens, the three young men were enjoying their night on the town so much that they had forgotten the desk clerk's words. It was only when they returned to a dark lobby that they remembered his warning. Well, there was nothing to do now but walk up the stairs! They decided that it would be best to tell each other stories along the way, which they did.

As they trudged up flight after flight, at the landing of the 33rd floor, two thirds of the way still remaining, the second sardar said he had an excellent story, but he would only reveal it when there was a suitable climax. And so they kept climbing, until they finally reached their floor. At which point the second sardar said that the room key was with the front desk.

There was no option but to descend the stairs to pick up the key. Once again they commenced telling stories to make the journey easier. When they had reached the 66th floor, the third sardar spoke up, 'I, too, have an interesting story. But I am only going to share it at the end.'

Finally, they were down at the ground floor. As they approached the front desk, the third sardar said, 'I had the key in my pocket all along!'

So it began all over again, another ascent of a hundred stories, in more ways than one. At the 50th floor, the first sardar's face lit up as though he had remembered something. 'Oye, I also have a story. But I will tell it only when we reach the top!'

In good time and a good deal more tired, they reached the 100th floor. The other two looked at the first sardar, who said, 'Oye, did you know, we're in the wrong tower; our hotel is actually on the other side of the street?'

Commentary

Such competitive idiocy is much the norm in many aspects of daily experience. The quest for personal thrill or recognition frequently trumps the general good, or even, quite often, one's own well-being. Of course, in this particular tale, the lingering effects of alcohol can hardly be discounted altogether. At least the antics of these three sardars are limited in their impact to just the three of them. Rather identical impulses on the part of many world leaders result in decades of devastation in unseen places and untold lives.

Fire-vire, Rescue-miscue

Santa Singh and Banta Singh successfully brought five men out alive from inside a burning house. Instead of being decorated for their efforts, they were booked by the police.
 Why?
 The five men they brought out were firefighters who were inside tackling the blaze.

Commentary

The Punjabi saying (quoted by the late Sardar Khushwant Singh from the back of a Delhi autorickshaw) says it all: *'Neki kar, chhitter kha'*. It literally means, 'Do good, get a shoe-beating'.

A Total Success

Mr and Mrs Banta Singh were staring at their son's school report card for the umpteenth time. No matter how many times one looked, it was difficult to discover anything in it to occasion joy. Despite Jeeto engaging special tutors, whose value Banta had always considered dubious and whose expense exorbitant, the boy had succeeded in doing badly across the board.

The report card read as follows (all scores in percentage):

English	13
Maths	11
Geography	10
Science	07
Social Studies	21
Economics	09
Hindi	16
Total	87

The mother was inclined to look on the positive side. '*Still ji, total'ch munde de number ainne kh'raab vi ni ne* (The boy's marks in total aren't so bad),' she said plaintively to Banta.

'*Oh vi ikko subjact jiddi ^&%$^ tuition ni laayi hoyi si* (That too the only subject for which we hadn't engaged any ^&%$^ tuition),' Banta remarked, shaking his head ruefully.

Commentary

The last figure is deliberately misleading: it is hard to imagine that it indicates 87 as a percentage. Nevertheless, it is true that each of us tries to take from any situation what is most supportive of our own preconceptions. Inertia is a term from Newtonian physics for a tendency of a body to persist in its current velocity, resisting change. It applies as much to human thought patterns. Most of us look for evidence to support what we already 'know'. The few who are able to take things as they are and discard what they know based on new input are the ones that change the world.

Not the Aam Aadmi

Banta Singh climbs up on to a comfortable branch on an Alphonso mango tree laden with fruit. Just as he is settling down, a monkey on an adjacent branch notices the competition and yells out, 'Why have you come up here, for heaven's sakes?'

'To eat an apple,' answers Banta.

'Are you nuts? Don't you know this is a mango tree?' the monkey shoots back.

'*Main tah eppal naal lai aaya vaan* (I've brought the apple with me),' Banta replies, displaying a Golden Delicious with a triumphant smile.

Commentary

'Not all those who wander are lost,' writes Tolkien. He might add, 'Not all who climb mango trees do so for mangoes.' Joy comes from purposeless activities, it is success that requires planning and plotting. The monkey cannot fathom why a human being should risk life and climb shimmying up a tree, especially without a desire to pluck fruit. In a way, the story reiterates literally Krishna's admonition in the Gita about being unconcerned with the fruits of one's actions. The physicist and teacher Richard Feynman captured the same idea in his inimitable style, 'Physics is like sex: sure, it may give some practical results, but that's not why we do it.' The art of effortless joy is a vanishing commodity in an age where planning, purpose, efficiency and success (as denoted by accumulation), etc. are the watchwords.

Great Expectations

Banta Singh was downcast, this much was obvious to anyone who saw him that week. His mood had steadily worsened day after day and when the weekend rolled around, it was almost as if he were clinically depressed. His friend and colleague Bachittar was surprised at this, especially considering what he knew. He caught up with Banta, and suggested going out for some coffee.

'Oye Bante,' he began when they had both sat down at the coffee shop. 'If anyone should be walking around with a smile, that should be you. Man...talk about Fortune shining! Three weeks ago, you got a big promotion. Two weeks ago, your uncle died leaving you his farmhouse. And just last week, you got a letter saying you'd won the lottery. One lucky guy! And now you're going about with this mournful munh... Oye, what happened?'

Banta shook his head sadly and remained silent awhile. Then he replied softly, 'Nothing happened...that's the problem... All this week and nothing!'

Commentary

'What brings happiness?' is a question that has engaged mankind practically through its entire history. It seems clear enough that there is nothing absolute about happiness. Is there a qualitative difference, between the emotions of the corporate tycoon who has successfully acquired a rival company and those of a little kid who has gotten his mother to buy him a shining plastic trinket from a street vendor? The joke illustrates the fleeting nature of any solace from without, but even more, shows up the role of expectation in causing pain. Like the stock market, the human mind also defines its wins and losses based on expectations. And like the market, Banta has already 'factored in' his gains of the last few weeks—by that definition, the absence of any windfall this week is tantamount to ill luck.

Theorisingh

His tour had taken him all over South India, and Banta Singh had come back to Amritsar with a deep love of filter coffee, masala dosa, gongura pickle, bisi bele bhath and several other food specialties from the region. At a 'welcome home' party thrown by his friend Santa Singh, he regaled a rapt audience with a slideshow of various sights and scenes including the Marina Beach, numerous temples, colourful dresses, etc.

Answering some questions after the slideshow, Banta was asked by someone, *'Oye Bante, Madrasi saare de saare kaale honde ne* (Are all Madrasis dark complexioned)?'

Banta had himself given the matter sufficient thought

during his tour and was thus able to reply confidently, *'P'aaji, aist'raan hai, uthhe loki baghair sunscreen lotion la ke saara din Sun TV, Surya TV de samne baithe rainde ne... ais kar ke...* (Brother, it's like this, many people over there spend all day watching Sun TV, Surya TV[32], and without wearing any sunscreen lotion. As a result...)'

Commentary

The obsession with skin colour is all too real in India. Matrimonial ads emphasize attractiveness with a well-known term, 'wheat-ish complexion'. The airwaves are full of well-known film and other personalities (men and women) hawking skin whitening products.

The Physic of Relativity

The little boy was obviously not feeling good. He was coughing, his eyes were crusty, he looked like he might have fever. The nurse in the waiting room took one look at the little fellow and immediately asked Banta to bring him inside so they could get the boy's vital signs and ready him to be examined by the doctor. Banta gently

---

[32]Surya TV and Sun TV are channels in South Indian languages

carried the child in his arms as he walked through the door to the consulting room. After somehow taking the temperature, which was itself quite a task because the boy was in distress and thus irritable, the nurse wanted to take his weight next. Try as they might, the boy did not want to be put on the scale, and clung to Banta Singh, wailing at the slightest sign of being set down from Banta's arms. The nurse considered the situation.

'How about we do this, Mr Singh? You keep your son in your arms and get on the weighing scale. Then I can hold your son while we take your weight alone. That way we can subtract and get your son's weight?,' she smiled. Banta thought it over and shook his head. 'Sorry sister, that won't work,' he said with a grimace. 'You see, he's not really my son...he is my nephew.'

Commentary

The joke uses an extreme exaggeration to make a relevant point. In domains with which we are not familiar or comfortable, we are unable to see and use techniques and strategies that might seem obvious to someone more conversant with the setup. To most people, a visit to the doctor is a black box. The doctor examines the patient, prescribes medicines, and that is that. The professional's word is sacrosanct—and to be taken literally. The interaction with the nurse too falls into this category.

Not Such a Long Journey

The train was about to leave when an elderly Sardarji got into the compartment, dragging a heavy suitcase after him. He sat down to catch his breath. The train jolted into motion, causing the suitcase to fall on its side, hitting the shin of the young fellow seated facing him. The sardar was most contrite, apologizing over and over. The youngster sitting opposite was gracious, and offered to put the suitcase away under the seat.

'No, no, no, young man,' boomed the sardarji. 'Please don't take the trouble. I have to get down at the next stop.'

The passenger on the right smiled. 'Oh, that's where I am getting down too. Are you from Surat then, Sardarji?'

'No, no, I am from Delhi, going to Bombay.'

'Sir, but I thought you were going to get down at Surat,' asked the young man, puzzled.

'Yes, but I will be taking the next train from Surat to Valsad. Then from Valsad to Vapi. Finally, from Vapi to Bombay.'

There was silence in the entire compartment. The sardar's answer had drawn the attention of every occupant in the vicinity. After a lull, the young man made bold to ask, 'Sir, but...but...this train goes all the way from Delhi to Bombay...why didn't you...'

The sardarji could well appreciate his confusion.

'Oye puttar, you see, I'm a heart patient. My doctor

has strictly forbidden me from making any long journeys,' he explained with a smile.

Commentary

I think the joke is brilliant. At one level the sardarji has captured the entire spirit behind differential calculus, the world of the small and infinitesimal. He has used the concept of modularity, the antidote to the pitfalls of monolithic design. At another level, he has circumvented some killjoy medic by redefining the long journey into multiple small ones. With Alfred Lord Tennyson, he echoes the aged Ulysses:
> How dull it is to pause, to make an end,
> To rust unburnish'd, not to shine in use!
> As tho' to breathe were life!

And, if he is taking his time in each stop, well, who could deny that the journey itself might be a rejuvenation in its own right?

Friends, Romans, Countrymen, Lend Me Your Legs!

Banta Singh was researching the topic of human voice communication with the common fire ant. After weeks of training, he had successfully taught a couple of specimens to respond when he yelled, 'Run!' Usually, after a couple of attempts aided sometimes by a sharp tap on the surface where it had been placed, the ant could be expected to scurry, proof of response to human voice commands, according to the paper Banta was writing.

His colleague Santa Singh was no slouch either. Watching Banta's experiments, he too began training a couple of fire ants, and was soon able to replicate Banta's results. One day, he decided to modify the experiment. He cut off the hind legs of the ant. When he yelled, 'Run,' the ant would still do as directed using the other four legs. He then removed the front legs and tried again, finding the ant still moving on his yelling. Finally, he took off the remaining two legs. When he yelled now, the ant moved no longer.

After trying this experiment over and over, he was ready to publish his path-breaking conclusion: 'Solenopsis fugax's hearing is via legs'.

Commentary

The joke points to two things, one a sad reality, and the other a happier but barely recognized scientific truth. The first is the widely prevalent practice of unnecessary vivisection in the name of science. Millions of animals, birds, amphibians and insects are subject to the most horrific cruelties, in laboratories and research facilities that present an outward impression of benign scientific excellence.

As to an insect 'hearing' through its legs, this is in fact quite believable. As human beings, we tend to apply our own modes of sensory input to every species. We forget that all sensory input ultimately leads to and is processed by the brain. Many animals have a very limited vision but a sense of smell or hearing might compensate to provide what human beings get primarily through their eyes. More to the point, this article[33] from *Science News* actually corroborates Santa's discovery:

'Biologists have long realized that ants can hear with their knees, picking up vibrations humming through leaves or nests or even the ground'.

Past Tense

Banta Singh was frustrated. He almost had the test aced. This one last question on the English paper was bothering him. He had a vague feeling he knew the answer, it was on the tip of his tongue, but he couldn't quite remember it. Adding to the tension, the time was up, and the teacher was approaching, collecting answer sheets. Banta quickly wrote down an answer and handed his paper to the teacher. He shook his head as he picked up his backpack

---

[33] http://tinyurl.com/kw86gx4

and headed out of the exam hall.

His friends were outside, discussing the test. '*Ik swaal da mainnu answer yaad ni aaya* (I couldn't remember the answer to one question): 'What is the past tense of think?,' he told them. 'I thought and thought but I couldn't get it. Finally, I just guessed and wrote down, "thunk"!'

Commentary

All of us have experienced brain freeze. You see somebody you know, but all of a sudden you cannot remember his name. It is not, you realize, a matter of effort. Paradoxically, the harder you try to remember it, the farther away it gets. When you are tense, the brain seems to miss even the most obvious things. Computer programmers will tell you stories of how they had sat up all night tearing their hair out over an intractable bug, and then gone home in frustration, only to return the following morning to see the answer staring them in the face. The same goes with the physical. The body is at its most alert when not tense. The finest slip fielders in cricket may appear to be taut, but they are not tense. For the reflexes to act, the muscles need to be loose, not tight.

Aw Shaqqs![34]

It was nothing specific, but Banta Singh, for the past couple of months, had been wondering if his wife wasn't playing around with some other guy. He hesitated to say anything without proof, and was going crazy bottling up the doubt and anger. His one source of calm and comfort in these rough times of emotional upheaval was his old buddy, Santa Singh, a confirmed bachelor with plenty of time to entertain his friend for drinks and conversation.

After a couple of beers one evening at Santa's place, Banta excused himself to the restroom. To say he was shocked by what he saw there would be an understatement. For, on a clothesline inside hung a couple of what are politely called 'unmentionables', a.k.a. female apparel of an intimate variety. He was convinced he had caught his wife's lover; but he just could not digest the idea that it was his dearest friend.

He flung the bathroom door open and stormed out yelling at Santa, 'Oye ^&%$^, *tere vallon eh ummeed ni si* (You ^&%$^, I did not expect this from you). With my wife? *Aa ki hai, dass* (What is this, tell me)?' He had grabbed Santa by the collar and virtually dragged him to the bathroom, pointing to the telltale items on the clothesline.

Santa stared at the evidence in shameful silence. Then

---
[34]'Shaqq' meaning 'doubt'

he said, hesitantly, '*Par p'aaji...tuhannu tah pataa hai...pabhi ji kadi ni underviyar paande* (But brother...as you know... sister-in-law never wears an underwear).'

Relief flooded Banta's face, followed by contrition. '*Oye, sahi gal hai. So sorry, yaar, main kham o'kha tere utte shaqq kitta* (Hey, that's right. So sorry, old pal, I needlessly suspected you).'

Commentary

Another case of 'not enough evidence to convict', also sometimes referred to as 'clean chit'.

A Matchless Record

Everybody knew of Banta Singh's reputation. A diligent and conscientious soul, he was in charge of the storeroom. Such was his passion for quality that he would check every single piece of equipment that entered his custody. One winter evening, when it was already dark, the power went out and the boss called out to Banta to fetch a box of matches so he could light some candles. Banta brought one immediately. Five minutes later the boss called out, saying that none of the matches appeared to work.

'*M'loom ni kyun, sirjee* (Don't know why, sir),' Banta replied. 'Every single one of them works. *Oye g'rantee e saddi* (I give my guarantee). I have personally tested them.'

Commentary

Okay, so every country conducts nuclear tests. But when push comes to shove, er...which is to say, conventional comes to nuclear, can you guarantee that the bomb will actually go off? This is the sort of dilemma which keeps every equipment manufacturer and user awake at night. There is no absolute certainty, but equipment-testing using statistical random sampling and other means is a constantly evolving area of research. No measurement (including testing) can be done without disturbing the system under examination. This is a principle emphasized in sources as diverse as physics textbooks and Chairman Mao's 1937 treatise, 'On Practice'. The latter uses a familiar example, 'If you want to know the taste of a pear, you must change the pear by eating it yourself,' thereby conflating testing with tasting, something social historians might want to keep in mind while explaining Mao's outsize influence in Bengal. In single-use products, use-testing can only be of samples, not every single unit. Banta just went overboard; had he simply checked one or two matchsticks out of every box—and discarded them, all would have been well.

The Ghost Who Drives[35]

It was a dark and stormy night, windy and rainy. Visibility was literally just a few feet. Banta Singh was stranded on a lonely road, several miles away from home. He was hoping some vehicle would come by and he might hitch a ride. As he walked slowly and cautiously along the side of the road, he was happy to see a pair of headlights approaching. He waved his arms frantically. The car slowed down and then stopped briefly. Yelling a quick thanks, he opened the door and hopped into the rear seat. Shutting his eyes and saying a quick prayer, he

---

[35] A reference to the popular comic hero of old, Phantom

said 'thank you so much' to the driver. It was only when he realized that the driver had not even acknowledged his thanks that he looked up.

There was no driver in the car, which had picked up a little speed and was now moving towards a curve in the road a few feet in front. Shock and fear surged through Banta's entire being. Petrified, he could not even scream, and could only pray silently. Suddenly, as he watched in terror through the fog, a hand reached in and turned the steering wheel to avoid going off the road. The car kept moving. There was no driver but the same hand seemed to know exactly when to come in and steer. Banta had always maintained an ambiguous attitude toward the truth about ghosts. Now, he knew the stories he had heard were all real. He waited not an instant more. Opening the door he tumbled out, then, scrambling to his feet, ran for his dear life, not stopping until he reached the nearest habitation.

It happened to be a bar.

Rushing in, he collapsed. The bartender and a couple of customers lifted him up, seated him in a chair and made him drink some brandy. When he was fit enough to say anything, he spluttered, 'ghost...ghost...car...' It was some time before he could talk, but when finally he was able to share his terrifying tale, the entire bar was listening in complete fascination.

At this point a couple of men, hair dishevelled and clothes dripping, staggered into the bar. As soon as they saw Banta holding court, one of them exclaimed to the other, 'Hey look, this is the idiot who jumped into the car when we were pushing it!'

Commentary

Context drives construction. Any situation is capable of an infinity of interpretations. Occam's razor advises that it is best to choose the most direct and simple explanation, the one that requires the least number of assumptions. But experience suggests that the razor is daily blunted; we are far more apt to swallow the most fantastic explanations in preference to the obvious and the straightforward.

High and Dry

It had taken every ounce of his powers of persuasion for Banta Singh, the film's director, to convince the hero to go through with it. The scene required a jump from a 15-foot-high diving board into the swimming pool. Ever since seeing the script, the hero had been kicking up a protest. Not only was he afraid of heights, he kept saying, he couldn't swim either. It had taken hours of pep talk from Banta, telling him to keep eyes shut till he reached the diving board, then keep his head straight and not look down into the pool as he walked to the end.

Somehow, all his cajolery had paid off, and the hero now stood at the edge of the board, striking a well-practiced diver's stance. As he looked straight ahead, he yelled out to Banta, 'Director sahib, please remember, I can't swim, somebody will have to be ready to rescue me.'

Banta smiled confidently, as befitting one who has already taken care of the matter. 'Oye, no problem, puttar', he yelled back. 'There's no water in the swimming pool!'

Commentary

Sometimes when a solution seems too simple, it really is!

Round-off Error

Banta Singh was new to the city, it was his first visit to his cousin. In the village, the only sports he had played or known were kabaddi, kushti, running races, etc. Cricket, soccer and the like were unknown to him. It was with a great deal of excitement, therefore, that his cousin had purchased tickets for the evening soccer match at the big stadium. He was looking forward to explaining the finer points of the game to Banta. How often did someone get to introduce another to soccer!

Banta Singh too was enjoying everything about the stadium as they waited for the game to start. Once it began, he was a little aghast to see a crowd of grown men kicking a ball from one side of the field to another.

'*Pra, aa ki kar rahe ne* (Brother, what's this they're doing),' he whispered to his host.

'*Doven teaman ball nu lathhan la'a la'a ke goal karna chahunde ne* (Both teams are kicking the ball, wanting to score a goal),' the cousin said, by way of a telegraphic introduction to soccer.

Banta wondered about his cousin's sanity, '^&%$^ *ehna da damaag kharaab hai? Ball tah pehle ton hi gol hai* (Are the ^&%$^ out of their minds? The ball is gol as it is)!'

Commentary

Gol means round or circular in Hindustani. Though it doesn't work in English translation, the original Punjabi literally amounts to saying, 'make the ball goal'. Being a practical individual, impatient with meaningless activity, Banta sees no point working on an objective which has already been achieved.

Safety ~~First~~ Fast

A car was seen speeding through the city streets one night. It did not stop at traffic lights, nor did it slow down for approaching vehicles. And its headlights were off too. Naturally, it was only a matter of time before this attracted the attention of a traffic policeman, who put on the sirens and lights on his motorbike to give chase. The car did not stop immediately but did do so at long last, slowing to a halt over several hundred feet.

The cop walked over to the driver's side, alert for any eventuality. His manner was grim. 'Your name?' he said.

It was Banta Singh.

'Do you realize you don't have your lights on, and you're driving at breakneck speed. Are you drunk or something?'

'Oh yes, I know my headlights are fused, sirjee. Not

only that, my brakes aren't working either. That's why I'm trying to get home as fast as I can, before I meet with an accident.'

Commentary

Banta is treating the 'accident' as an external event scheduled for a specific time in the future, making it imperative to reach a place of safety prior to that time. Here, his own actions are likely to cause the accident! It offers an instructive view into two categories of problems: the ones caused or enabled by our own actions or neglect, and the others that are outside our control. It is true that being better prepared and organized in general helps avoid or deal with external problems. For example, an electrical power cut or a flat tire are unpredictable external happenings. Still, the person who keeps candles and matches, or the person who knows how to fix a spare tire, can cope with these incidents better than someone who does not. The cartoonist and author Scott Adams has an interesting observation on this matter.[36] People who have systems generally do better than people who have goals, which is to say, people who do the right things over a long run increase the probability of success more than people who merely have the right aims.

---

[36]http://dilbert.com/blog/entry/goals_vs_systems/

Wife Insurance

Santa Singh had come from abroad to visit his best friend Banta Singh who was ailing. Santa and Banta both knew that this was the final goodbye; the doctors had given Banta no more than a few days.

Softly, Santa asked his friend, '*Oye, ik gal mainnu dasseen* (Hey, tell me something). You told me you had cancer. But the entire neighbourhood seems to think you have AIDS? *Gal ki hai* (What's going on)?'

The reply was slow and halting, but accompanied by a sly wink, '*Oye, cancer tah hai* (It is cancer, all right). But I don't want the guys hitting on my beautiful wife after I'm gone.'

Commentary

A brilliant strategy such as it is. Graham Greene noted that whenever someone called on the phone and left you a message saying it was important, it was fairly certain that the message was more important to them than it was to you. Adam Smith visualized an enlightened self-interest on the part of individuals as an invisible hand regulating society. An appeal to self-interest (and one to self-preservation is bound to be several times as persuasive) is likely to fall on more receptive ears than one merely based on morality, righteousness and what not.

DeMOBilisingh

The interview was a long and tedious ordeal. This was as it should be, for it was to select the police chief of a district rife with social tensions, industrial strikes and agrarian unrest, all in equal measure.

It was a position which entailed dealing with protesters practically every day.

'So, Mr Singh,' the chair of the panel asked Banta. 'If you were faced with an angry crowd intent upon some form of confrontation so as to make news, how would you go about dispersing the assembly? Keep in mind that the media is right there, likely to report any use of force as police brutality.'

Banta Singh thought about it for a minute. Then he replied, 'Sirjee, I think I would begin by soliciting contributions for the orphanage building fund.'

Commentary

Banta Singh is proving once again to be an adept in human psychology. Nothing dissolves a gathering more quickly than an impending request for charity.

An Eye for Detail

Many years before the interview described in the previous joke, there was Banta Singh's hiring into the police force. Here too there was a momentous interview.

Banta and a couple of other potential candidates had been shortlisted for a lone entry-level position in the police. The interviewer took out from his desk drawer a profile photograph of a wanted criminal. He placed it in front of them and asked them to study it.

He asked the first candidate, 'How would you go about tracking this badmash[37]?'

The candidate replied, 'Sirjee, very easy. I will look for a man who has only one eye!'

The interviewer pursed his lips but said nothing. He asked the second candidate, 'How about you?'

The second candidate answered eagerly, 'No problem, sir. He is a one-eyed man with only a left ear and no right...'

The interviewer felt his heart sinking. He was fast losing any hope of finding a suitable detective. Turning to Banta, he asked without enthusiasm or expectation, 'You?'

Banta did not answer immediately, but thought for a full two minutes. He then replied, 'This man wears a contact lens.'

The interviewer was shocked. Indeed it was true that

---

[37] Of a bad profession, infamous

the criminal was short-sighted and preferred contacts over spectacles! How in the name of tarnation had this young chap figured all this out so quickly? This guy was simply brilliant. Thanking the two other candidates for their interest in the job, he dismissed them and immediately offered Banta Singh the position.

In later years, whenever asked how he had deduced that bit about the contact lenses, Banta was always modest, 'Oye, it was simpal. How could a guy with only one ear ever wear spectacles?'

Commentary

In his interview, Banta had willy-nilly applied Sherlock Holmes to good effect, 'It is an old maxim of mine that when you have excluded the impossible, whatever remains, however improbable, must be the truth.' Maybe he should've also listened to this from the world's most famous detective, 'I am afraid that I rather give myself away when I explain. Results without causes are much more impressive.'

The Show Must Go On

Visiting the Mughal Gardens in Delhi, a foreign visitor could not help but be transfixed by an extraordinary tableaux. Ahead of him were two sardars, engaged in a variety of gardening which he, a lifelong gardener, could simply not understand. One sardar would dig a small hole in the ground, piling up the earth to the side. He would then move a foot to the right and begin digging a similar hole. Meanwhile, the second sardar would simply fill the previous hole with all the earth which had been piled up next to it. The same thing with the next hole, and the one after, and the one after that.

The foreigner watched about ten repetitions of this performance before he decided he needed to learn something about this seemingly remarkable feature of Indian horticulture. He slowly made his way towards the two sardars. Apologizing for disturbing them, he endeavoured, politely in broken Hindustani, to ask what they were doing. The first sardar replied that they were engaged in seasonal planting. 'Dahlias and tulips,' the second sardar helpfully added.

'But...I didn't see you plant anything,' the foreigner ventured, partly in awe. His mind was swimming with visions of Indian mysticism, of swamis producing fruits out of their bare hands, of yogis staying buried for weeks...

His question was being answered. '*Oye, aist'raan haiga eh sirjee* (Sir, it's like this). These days we are all modernized and work on assembly-line principles,' the first sardar began. 'We are three people in a team. I am Banta Singh; I do the digging. Then there is Bachittar Singh, who does the planting. Finally,' he said, pointing to the other sardar, 'this is Santa Singh, who does the filling up.'

'Today, our colleague Bachittar is out on leave. But as you know, the work, or the planting season, doesn't stop for anybody. So we are continuing with our duties,' Santa Singh concluded.

Commentary

Admiral Horatio Nelson is credited with the famous line, 'England expects that every man will do his duty.' By this reckoning, Banta and Santa are being exemplary. The trouble begins when the notion of duty gets so narrowly defined as to forget any larger purpose. Graduating from the compartmentalized performance of the task to its constant integration with overall objective is the first step, perhaps, in an executive direction. The lower down executive thinking can be pushed, the more successful in general will be the organization, so long as excellence in the performance of duty is not compromised. In the military, there is a distinct gap between those who reason and issue orders, and those for whom it is not to reason but only to do and die. The same Nelson is also quoted as saying, '...you must always implicitly obey orders, without attempting to form any opinion of your own regarding their propriety,' reflecting exactly that ethos.

Disposingh

A sardar's office computer was beginning to cause daily problems. It was slow, sometimes it would hang, at other times it would take forever to save something; using it had become an unpleasant experience overall. The company's tech-support was called in, finally, and the young man pronounced that it was all because the hard disk had very little room left. He suggested that all unwanted files be sent to the trashcan to free up space.

For the next two days, the sardarji was busy moving things to the trashcan. Three things resulted. One, three office printers ran out of ink. Two, the paper supply in the office was nearly empty. Three, he got a memo for violating the office policy on recycling paper instead of throwing it into the trash. What did not result? Any improvement in performance of the computer!

Commentary

The Sardarji had printed out all the unwanted files and put them into the physical trashcan. A less environmentally damaging version of this joke has him making a copy of every file before deleting it.

Either way, it is a comment on the amount of junk we accumulate, as much in computers as in our garages, as much by way of data as by way of real things. The metaphor of printing out the junk files and physically disposing of them is also quite relevant. The burning of effigies each Dussehra is exactly along these lines—the inner demons which we are supposed to exorcise in this fashion well survive the fiery fanfare with which Ravana and his cohorts are dispatched. In a larger sense, the joke illustrates the futility of trash disposal in an era where the creation of trash, extolled as the growth rate of the economy, occupies an iconic pedestal perhaps unrivalled by the gods of old.

No Guessingh

Banta: 'Oye Sante, thailey'ch ki lai ja riha hain (Hey Santa, what are you carrying in that bag)?'

Santa: 'Ande... Je kinne ande haigain sahi gass kar liya taan main tainnu dohenn dai davaanga (Eggs... If you can guess how many, I'll give you both of them)!'

Banta: (after thinking a few minutes), 'Oye yaar, bande nu ^&%$^ ik hint tah dai de (Hey, at least you could give this chap a ^&%$^ hint).'

Commentary

'There was a gate, but as a general thing he was too crowded for time to make use of it.' (*The Adventures of*

Tom Sawyer.)

Conditioned by the everyday trickeries of the world, people are apt to be leery about something that appears too easy.

So too with tests and examinations, where as a rule, the obvious is obviously a red herring. Decades ago, a friend of mine was appearing for his National Science Talent Scholarship interview.

Hanging on the wall, behind the interviewers, was a photograph of a bearded man with long hair. My friend had instantly recognized him to be Rabindranath Tagore. And as if on cue, the first question to him was, 'Who is that in the photograph?' no doubt intended to put the young aspirant at ease.

But the young aspirant's mind was whirling with complicated conundrums. Why would they be asking such a simple question, and in the final round of a prestigious national contest? Besides, what on earth did Tagore: poet, writer, artist, have anything to do with science? He made up his mind.

'Homi J. Bhabha,' he answered confidently, giving the name of an eminent Indian scientist whose face he did not recognize, who was clean-shaven and wore his hair short!

Outthinking the Enemy

It was that season again. Every man, woman and child in town was troubled by mosquito bites each night as they slept. An array of techniques, some ancient, some ultramodern, were daily being pressed into service in this struggle. It was in this context that a friend was surprised to hear Banta Singh make the declaration that he had come up with a winning strategy against the mosquitoes.

'*Oye, main tah unhaan naal mantal game khedaanga* (I'm going to play with their heads, a mental game),' he told his friend.

The friend was curious, naturally. Banta explained his plan.

'*Draaying room'ch coil ch'laavaanga. Saare ^&%$^ machhar jang othhe hai samajh ke draaying room'ch chale jaange. Assaan ^&%$^ 'raam naal bedroom'ch kharrate maar-maarke sovaange* (I'll run the mosquito coil in the drawing room. All the ^&%$^ mosquitoes will rush there, thinking that's where the battle is! Meanwhile, I'll be off snoring comfortably in the bedroom).'

Commentary

Substitute 'mosquito' with 'Al Qaeda', 'drawing room' with 'Iraq' and 'bedroom' with 'America', and hey presto, doesn't Banta Singh seem automatically to morph into George W. Bush?

President Bush's proposition that 'we are fighting them there (Iraq) so that we don't have to fight them here (America)' is almost a replica of Banta Singh's idea.

Over the Limit

Mrs Banta Singh had knitted the sweater with much love and affection. It contained his favourite colours, in a beautiful herringbone weave. And just as he liked, it was a cardigan not a pullover. A pocket on each side would enable him to hook his thumbs as she had seen the hero do in her favourite TV series. She blushed a little as she visualized him wearing it and leaning roguishly against the doorway. And my, the dollar-size brass buttons were just so elegant. He would be pleased. Would he? She sure hoped so, for she had poured her heart and soul into this project to make sure she could ship it to him in time for his birthday. She set off to the post office to mail it.

When Banta Singh received the package from his wife, he was absolutely delighted. Ripping the parcel open, he was thrilled and moved to tears at the obvious pains his wife had gone to. The cardigan was perfect. Holding it out in front of him, he swore to himself he would wear it as long as he lived. It was then that he noticed it had no buttons.

Just at that moment his phone rang. 'Did you get something by post?' a shy voice on the other end trailed off.

'*Soniye, svaeter barha changa hai* (Darling, the sweater is very beautiful),' he began, continuing on with various expressions of endearment and thanks. Finally he asked, '*Par...tu button laana p'uhl gayi* (But...did you forget to put the buttons)?'

'Oh, that's what I was going to tell you. The post office wale said the buttons weighed too much and would double the price of postage. So I decided to take them off. You'll find them packed separately inside the package.'

Commentary

The joke is a beautiful illustration of the concept of a closed system. No matter how things are distributed inside of the parcel, the weight is going to be the same. To Mrs Banta Singh, the fact that the sweater weighed too much implied that she could correct the problem by taking the buttons off the sweater. It is an apt metaphor for a spectrum of social pathologies arising out of petty cleverness, a blithe confidence that eternal truths can be bypassed by means of technological artifice and legerdemain. Chief among these is the belief that economic growth stands by itself without regard to environmental consequences. Some of our ancients seem to have had a far better grasp of the nature of closed systems than the tech-besotted zombies of our times, as these lines from Gulzar's 1979 film, *Meera*[38], based on the life of Meerabai (1498–1557), would indicate:

Rana ji mai to govind ke gun ga su.
Raja ruthe, nagri rakhe,
Hari ruthe kahan ja su?

(Translation)
Your Majesty, I prefer to sing praises of the Lord (i.e. rather than of the king).
Should king lose his temper, the public may yet preserve (me),
If God should lose his, where would I go?

Making the Connection

Banta Singh and his friend Santa Singh are enjoying an evening samosa and chai at a roadside dhaba, watching the traffic go by. A large truck appears, towing another truck. They are connected by a stout rope.

Watching the slow progress of the two trucks, Banta shakes his head sadly and remarks to his friend, '*Main kainna ajj kal lokaan da damagh vi kharaab ho gaya hai. Oye, tu ni*

---

[38]Sung by Vani Jairam, music by Pt Ravishankar; https://www.youtube.com/watch?v=ZoaTeB-gS7E

*vekh'ya, ik chhotta jiha rassa lai jaan layi do-do vadde-vadde truck istimaal karde ne ^&%$^* (I say, these days people have gone bonkers. Did you see that, two big trucks to transport a tiny ^&%$^ piece of rope)!'

Commentary

Banta may be missing the point here, but he is making a larger one. We are so accustomed to viewing things from one standpoint that we cannot even conceive that there could be a different way of looking at them. Somebody once remarked that if a space alien were to look at New York City from the sky, he might be forgiven for concluding that its citizens were the automobiles, which appeared to consume and disgorge human beings from time to time. A paper[39] published in 1956 for the American Anthropological Association makes a brilliant example of this.

Something very similar to Banta Singh's view is precisely what started the courier service revolution. A student paper at Harvard looked at airline travel in reverse: instead of the luggage being an accompaniment to the passenger, a passenger became one to legitimize the transport of the real item of importance, the luggage. It was the idea that launched Federal Express.

---

[39]'Body Ritual among the Nacirema' by Horace Miner; https://www.msu.edu/~jdowell/miner.html

No Disguisingh

A donkey had kicked Banta Singh in the stomach. He was knocked down, and in severe pain. It was nearly a quarter of an hour before he recovered his full breath, and another quarter hour by the time the pain became tolerable. By this time the donkey had run away. Nothing deterred, Banta ran in the direction he had seen the donkey go. It took him a good part of that day and a fair portion of the next, but it was with a triumphant smile that he returned, pulling by a noose a protesting zebra from the touring circus.

'*Oye, mainnu ulloo banaunda e* ^&%$^ (Trying to make a fool of me, are you)!' he was yelling at the animal between thwacks. '*Soch'ya tracksuit pa lavenga tah main pehchaanan ga ni* (Did you think I wouldn't recognize you if you put on a tracksuit)?!'

Commentary

The joke is rather uncomfortably close to reality. As I write this, the Indian Supreme Court has just acquitted[40] a group of prisoners kept in prison for ten years on false charges. Detective work the world over appears to have

---

[40]"They asked me to choose: Godhra, Pandya or Akshardham', *Indian Express*, 21 May 2014

been overtaken by a desire for catching and convicting someone, somehow, and scoring well-publicized victories instead of bringing the actual perpetrator to justice.

Lavoisier Was Right!

Banta Singh is visiting an ailing acquaintance at the hospital. On seeing Banta, the patient appears to be overcome with emotion. All of a sudden he seems choked up and unable to speak. Tears streaming down his cheeks, he begins spluttering and gesticulating wildly.

Seeing his distress but unable to fathom all this sentiment at the sight of a casual visitor, Banta nevertheless has the presence of mind to hand him a paper and pen. The patient scrawls something and shoves the paper back at Banta, collapsing back on the bed even as he does so. In the ensuing melee of frantic doctors and nurses, Banta Singh stands petrified, watching them try to revive the man. In vain, unfortunately. They are unable to save the poor fellow.

It is only when he reaches home late that evening after the ceremonies, that he remembers the piece of paper. Fishing it out of his pocket, he looks at it. It reads, 'You are standing on my oxygen tube!'

Commentary

Zen masters emphasize the importance of mindfulness in all activity. We can understand why awareness of our motivations, words and actions, and their impact upon others around us, may be transformational.

H.L. Mencken wrote, 'The average man never really thinks from end to end of his life... My guess is that well over 80 per cent of the human race goes through life without having a single original thought'.

Far more tragic, and scary, is the prospect that modern life permits, nay forces, perfectly good people to cause enormous harm to other living things, even from thousands of miles away, by their lifelong mindlessness. The innocuous act of sitting with a few friends and chomping down on a hamburger in America is linked to the daily clearance of several acres of Amazon rainforest into farmland to raise fodder for beef cattle. A mindless (and non-stop) passage from one corporate sponsored thrill to the next constitutes the lives of an increasingly large number of people.

Drawing Conclusions

'What is that on your arm?' Banta Singh inquired of a young man coming out of the medical lab back into the reception area.

'Oh, that's where they stuck a needle into my vein to draw blood for my blood test,' the other replied, pointing to a bandage on a forearm with a tiny patch of red in the middle.

Banta's face acquired a look of pure terror. He burst into tears and began running towards the door. A couple of people waiting in the lobby stopped him to ask what had happened.

'Oye, they called me here for a urine test! *Jaan bachi taan lakkhaan paaye* (Thank heavens I escaped),' he explained before dashing out.

Commentary

Mental associations are powerful things. Banta had connected every kind of test with a needle, and the ensuing visions were understandably terrifying. But it is in the nature of the mind to make associations and to categorize without even being conscious of doing so. Long ago, new to the US, I was at an airport. Flanking a stairway in the middle were two escalators, one going up and the other coming down. I found myself wondering briefly why there weren't two staircases as well, before recognizing that I had just starred in my very own sardar joke!

Facsimile or Fax Ni Mili[41]?

The boss called for Banta Singh to come into his office. Handing him a file folder containing a sheet of paper, he said, 'Listen carefully. This is a top-secret agreement. I just signed it. Nobody is to know about it. I want you to secretly fax it to Mr Sharma, his fax number is... Remember once again, it is top-secret.'

Banta departed with suitable solemnity befitting the top-secret document he bore in his hands. He faxed it with due care, and returned the folder with the agreement back to the boss. While he was still in the boss's office, the phone rang. The boss picked up the phone. His face soon acquired a frown, and he kept saying, 'Hmm...hmm...' before concluding, 'give me a few minutes' and putting down the phone.

'Mr Sharma says the fax is blank,' he said to Banta. 'What did you do, fax it with the printed side up or something?'

'Oye, no no sirjee, I know how to send a fax.'

'Well, send it again,' said the boss, handing him the folder once again.

Banta sent off the fax once more and returned with the folder to the boss. The phone rang again. This time the boss was extremely apologetic to the other party. When he put the phone down, he turned to Banta and

---

[41]'*Ni mili*' meaning 'didn't get'

yelled, 'What the hell is happening? Same blank fax again.' He wondered if he had given an empty sheet to Banta by mistake. He opened the folder to look. The sheet was indeed the agreement, but it looked like it had been folded down the middle. 'Why has the paper been folded?,' the boss was curious.

'Sirjee, but you said it was top-secret. So naturally I folded the paper before faxing it,' was Banta's confident reply.

Commentary

Who knows but that Banta Singh was anticipating the days of electronic snooping and the need for encryption! Most people don't realize that the instantaneous communication they so cherish comes fraught with many possibilities for interception and unauthorized access. With the old-fashioned physical envelope, you could at least see that a letter had been tampered with. No such comfort in the case of fax, email, etc.

There is another aspect to Banta Singh's seeking to hide the document from the very recipient for whom it was intended. Such is the imperative of secrecy that things are hidden from the very people to whom they rightly belong. It is the hallmark of the national security age to have countless laws dotting the statute book, all in the name of protecting the population from itself. American senators tell us that they are horrified by the secret laws that exist, but can share no more with their supposed masters, the people.

A Stork Misapprehension

Even as the cellphone began to ring, Banta Singh knew it was time. Sure enough, it was Jeeto on the line. The baby was on its way.

'*Oye, tu koi fiqr na kar soniye, main hune auna* (Don't you worry, my darling, I'm coming over right away),' he reassured her in the gentlest tone.

True to his word, he was by his wife's side as soon as traffic would permit, having asked the taxi driver to wait outside as he rushed into the house. Slowly he escorted Jeeto to the waiting cab, settling her with great care into the back seat. He got in next to her, held her hand, while he took out his handkerchief and dabbed her perspiring forehead. Then he turned to the taxi driver and said, 'What are you waiting for? Domino's, and jaldi[42]!'

In all her agony, Jeeto could not help but mutter in perplexity, 'Which hospital is that?'

'It's just a new place around the corner,' he smiled at her. 'They're big on their free deliveries.'

Commentary

And they are indeed, of pizza. The old saying, 'there's a sucker born every minute' is true only because inside each

---

[42]Pronto, fast, quickly

human being is an irretrievable believer in deals too good to be true. In my early days in America, eyes peeled for the super sales everybody seemed to be talking about, I suddenly noticed a sign saying, 'Pants: $1, Shirts: $0.50'. I ran to my apartment to tell my friends. My joy and excitement were short-lived. A roommate brought me down to earth saying, 'You idiot, that must be a dry-cleaning shop.' It is true that once the rock-bottom prices captured my attention, I had registered nothing else.

Socket to 'em

It was the junior nurse who first thought it disturbing. She had noticed that every Sunday for the last four weeks, and just around midmorning, there had been some kind of crisis in the ICU. Now, a crisis in the ICU is hardly unexpected, but the regular pattern she found rather curious. She brought it to the attention of her supervisors, and pretty soon a regular investigation was on. A high-power team comprising doctors, nursing staff, administration, etc. swung into action.

It was several days before the team zeroed in on the cause.

It was discovered that Banta Singh, the new janitor whose duty fell on Sunday mornings, had the following standard operating procedure. He would enter the room, unplug something from the wall to plug-in his vacuum cleaner. After a quick clean, he would plug back the original device into the socket before going on to the next room.

Commentary

Perhaps a variant of the popular 'plug-and-play (with someone's life)'?

Glass Struggle

Banta Singh and Santa Singh had just gotten hired by a catering outfit. There was a big outdoor party the same evening, and a lot of work had to be done. Every member of the catering staff was stretched to the limit with not a second to idle.

A supervisor suddenly noticed that the guests needed water. Calling Banta and Santa, he asked them to go inside into the pantry where the glasses were kept, fill them with water and bring them out on the large trays they would also find in the pantry.

After examining each glass inside the pantry, Banta and Santa just could not help wondering what kind of catering business these people ran. They went back to the supervisor and Banta said, '*Oye, aithhe tah ^&%$^ ik vi gilaas kam da ni hai. Uppar ton saare de saare bandh ne te thalleyon khule* (Hey, there is not even a single ^&%$^ glass here that's of any use. Every single one is closed at the top and open at the bottom)!'

Commentary

Not just beauty but utility too is in the eyes of the beholder!

Dedusingh

The three friends would meet every Friday night at the usual adda[43], have a couple of drinks together and catch up on what was going on in each other's lives.

One Friday night, the first friend was in tears. 'I think it's over between me and my wife,' he said to the other two. 'I found a Postal Service mailbag under our bed a couple of days ago. And yesterday it was gone. She is having an affair with the postman.'

The other two commiserated with their buddy. But the very next week there was trouble once more.

---

[43]'Adda' meaning 'a meeting place'

'My misfortune this week,' began the second friend, stoically. 'I loved and trusted that woman. And with my car mechanic too. I was looking for my slippers this morning; peeping under the bed what do I find but the guy's overalls—with the sewn-in name tag for heavens' sake!'

They drowned the two friends' sorrows in drinks.

The very next Friday it was Banta Singh who was somber. 'Oye, guess what? My dog was barking at the bed. I look under, and what do you think I discover? A pint-size ^&%$^ real-life jockey, riding pants and all. Before I could catch him, the ^&%$^ jumped through the window and ran away.' He paused briefly to recover his breath before continuing.

'I'm absolutely convinced my wife is involved in some hanky-panky with a ^&%$^ horse.'

Commentary

'...and stop not till the goal is reached,' exhorts Vivekananda. Perhaps the Swami should've added, for Banta's benefit, that in ratiocination as in real life, one should stop when the goal is reached.

Birth Pang(a)s[44]

'Okay! Banta Singh, correct?,' the interviewer began, thumbing through Banta's resume.

Banta nodded, smiling.

'Very good...Banta, where were you born?' the interviewer continued, part of the preliminary, 'full toss' questions intended to put the candidate at ease.

'In Punjab,' replied Banta.

Though an Englishman, the interviewer had family connections with Punjab; his father and uncles had served there during the British times and he had grown up hearing about various towns and cities from the region. Genuinely curious now, he asked, 'Oh! Which part?'

Banta's face assumed a look bordering on derision. What a ridiculous query! This interviewer seemed to have lost it completely. He could not help being a little austere when he replied.

'Oye sirjee, all parts, of course.'

Commentary

To get the obvious element out of the way, the interviewer meant which part of the state, Banta Singh understood it as which part of himself.

---

[44]Provocation

The deeper aspect of the joke is reflected in the daily news of the challenges thrown up by immigration-heavy societies. A person may be born physically, even grow up, in one milieu, but might retain or reflect the values of a completely different one. All parts of the human being do not always reflect the ambient environment equally. It is said that the 9/11 hijackers, though committed to a religion based in Arabia, were entirely at home in the ways of the West. A survey conducted recently in the United Kingdom discovered that young men and women born and brought up in England were more adherent to the religion and values of their parents' birthplaces than even their parents themselves! The very term, 'a man of many parts', is used to describe someone who has multiple (positive) aspects. Indeed there is hardly any human being that is a single entity in this sense. This dilemma was expressed poignantly by a German who spoke of his country's Turkish immigrants and the problems with their integration, 'We thought we were getting workers, only to realize in time that we were also getting people.'

News Flash

'A twin-engine four-seater plane crashed due to bad weather last night in a graveyard in Punjab. Local sardars have recovered 235 bodies so far.'

Commentary

Whether this piece of sardonic humour matches a more serious observation is something you might want to consider. Nothing definite has been established regarding the disappearance of Netaji Subhas Chandra Bose, a hero of the Indian freedom struggle, subsequent to an air crash in the final days of World War II in 1945. For decades afterwards, competing speculations ran riot in India. Some said he had become an ascetic wandering in the Himalayas. Others claimed he was being held in the Soviet Union. Some believed he had been kept in custody with the knowledge of the Indian government post freedom. Quite widely, it was believed, particularly among people from his state of West Bengal, that he had survived the air crash. It led one Indian writer to muse that if you asked a Bengali a hundred years from now whether Netaji was still alive, he would answer in the affirmative.

The mass psyche much prefers the sensational, the grandiose, even the impossible, to the simple and straightforward.

A Trademark Issue

The young man on the train was about to tell this wonderful sardar joke he had heard. But it was just as he opened his mouth that he noticed a burly sardar in the upper berth of the adjoining cabin, well within earshot. It was too late now not to continue, having garnered the attention of his audience. Thinking on his feet, so to speak, he altered the joke, substituting Bihari for sardar. When he had finished, and the others were still laughing, the sardar jumped down from his perch above. Clearly, he was upset. He strode up to the joke teller and grabbed him by the collar. The shaking young fellow could say nothing. Teeth chattering, he waited for the blows to land.

None came. The sardar spoke, 'Bihari? Oye, ki hoya ^&%$^ ? Saare sardar mar gaye ne (Bihari? What the ^&%$^ happened? Did all the sardars die or something)?'

Commentary

Indeed. An iconic status is not something to be given up lightly. In the world of mental associations, branding is a vital activity. Capturing and retaining 'mind space'—registering an idea or a product inside the public consciousness, is the phrase popularized by Trout and Ries, authors of a landmark paper in marketing[45]. It is, according to them, the central challenge of the marketplace. The pre-eminent high ground in the arena of humour in India has long been the preserve of the sardar joke. The sardar in this joke is rightly being protective of this venerable trademark.

---

[45]'Positioning Cuts Through Chaos in the Marketplace', by Jack Trout and Al Ries, *Advertising Age*, 1 May 1972

Landless Labour

The flight was a half hour from landing in Bombay when the captain's voice crackled over the speakers, 'Nothing too serious, ladies and gentlemen, but we seem to have lost one engine, which means we will have to slow our descent into Mumbai by a half an hour.'

A half hour passed, and the captain spoke again. 'I don't mean to alarm you, ladies and gentlemen, but I do have to tell you that a second engine is also failing. We still have two engines left, all it means is we are going to land an hour late. Sit back, relax and enjoy the flight. Our flight attendants will do everything to make you comfortable.'

Banta Singh looked at his watch.

Another half hour in, it was the captain again, 'Ladies and gentlemen, I'm sorry to tell you that the third engine has also failed...' his voice trailing off.

Banta Singh turned to his neighbour and fuming, said, 'Oh My God, now if one more engine should fail, we'll be stuck in the air all day!'

Commentary

Of course you need the engine to land, but Banta forgets that you need the engine to stay up in the air too. To match our modern (or postmodern) lives, we tend to compartmentalize our thinking as well. Banta could just as soon have added, 'There goes my meeting!' Such hyper focusing on specific goals and objectives is the lesson taught everywhere, every day. The joke is a fine example of the absurdities that result from this process.

It's Malthus, You Phalthus[46]!

The lecturer was concluding his long but compelling presentation on the perilous increase of population, particularly as it related to India. He had shown a number of slides to provide a graphic illustration of the dire consequences of the nation's population explosion to both the environment and to human living conditions. He had saved the most telling statistic for the end.

'Someplace, somewhere, in India, there is a woman delivering a baby every 10 seconds,' he declared, pointing dramatically to the last slide, which had the same words in bold font.

The hall fell silent as the gathering slowly digested the enormity of this fact.

The lull was broken as a much moved Banta Singh rose slowly from his seat in the audience. Thumping the desk in front of him, he shook with emotion as he looked

---

[46]'Phaltu' meaning 'spare' or 'useless'

around the room and proclaimed, 'Ladies and gentlemen, what are we waiting for? We need to find and stop that woman immediately!'

Commentary

If the lecturer had said, 'There is a baby being born every 10 seconds somewhere in India,' Banta Singh would perhaps not have misunderstood. However, whether it is one woman or multiple women delivering babies, the addition to the population is exactly the same. The technique of identifying a range of data via a single sample is used frequently in science. For example, the centre of gravity of an object is really an abstract representation of every part of the object, notionally personified by one single point. If you want to alter the centre of gravity, it entails altering a real part of the object. In this sense, Banta's exclamation is justified. Finding and stopping that woman translates to communicating with all parts of the population to stem growth.

Password

The fellow waiting in line behind Banta Singh at the ATM decided to have some fun. As Banta finished using the machine and was putting the money into his wallet after counting it, he whispered to Banta, 'Hey, I saw your password.'

Banta could not believe this. He was always careful to cover the keypad with his left hand as he punched in the numbers with his right. 'Oye, that is impossible,' he said defiantly.

'Oh yes, I know exactly what it is. Isn't it star-star-star-star (****)?' said the man with a knowing smile.

'Oye, you are wrong. You don't know anything. It is 3764!' Banta snarled proudly as he left the booth.

Commentary

It can be argued that there are a few impulses more injurious to one's well-being than the urge to prove someone else wrong, and oneself right.

The In-laws of Relativity

Banta Singh looked forlorn as he said it. The sadness in his face only reflected the emotional turmoil raging within.

'*I'm sorry yaar Jeeto, main tainnu enna pyaar kardaan, enna pyaar kardaan, par ehna afsos, tere naal shaadi ni kar sakdaan* (I love you so, so, much, but sadly I can't marry you Jeeto).'

She looked devastated. Tears welled up in her eyes. '*Par kyon, ki hoya* (But why, what happened)?' she pleaded.

Banta knew he had to stay strong. Inside he was all jell-o.

'*Hunn kee karaan soniye* (Now what can I do, my darling)? But, *k'aar di parapara vi tah koi cheej hundi hai* (But family tradition needs to be considered too), and I don't want to be the one to break it... I've given this a lot of thought,' he began.

She had no idea what tradition he was referring to. She did not have to wait long.

'You see, in our house, for generations we've only married within our family. My dadaji is married to my dadiji, similarly, my nanaji to my naniji, my papaji to my mummyji, even in my own generation, my bhaiya is married to my bhabi, and my sister Jassi to my jijjaji.'

'Kaash, if only you had been related to me!'

Commentary

In his classic textbook on Economics, Paul Samuelson begins by cautioning against the post hoc fallacy, '*Post hoc, ergo propter hoc,*' being the full form in Latin, meaning simply, 'after this, hence because of this'. Banta Singh appears to have come up with a rider, his own contribution to Logical Theory, roughly, *post hoc, ergo pre hoc* (after this, hence before this).

Before you laugh too hard at Banta, however, do bear in mind that the daughter-in-law in many Indian families is expected to erase any memories of her connection with her birth family and integrate completely with that of her husband's. Anyone who fancies that this notion is a relic from a pre-cellphone era may correct this impression simply by sitting through a couple of Indian serials on television, where this exact idea gets reinforced every hour of the day.

But with or without social pressure, in a context where everyone in the family is thought of so much as a member of a duo (dadaji–dadiji, bhaiya–bhabhi, etc.) that their individual origins are forgotten, it is hardly surprising that Banta should view the act of marriage as incidental, almost forgettable, to the future inseparability of the two people concerned. In this deeper sense, Banta is only echoing Amir Khusrau, if clumsily:

Man tu shudam tu man shudi,
Man tan shudam tu jaan shudi.
Taa kas na goyad baad azeen,
Man deegaram tu deegari.

(Translation)
I have become you, you me,
I have become body, you soul.
So that no one can say hereafter,
That I am another, you another.

Signs of Trouble

'Arre yaar, you can do it,' the friend insisted. 'Besides, the money is not all that bad,' he added as a clincher. He was trying to persuade Banta Singh to take over for him while he was out of town for a day. The job, providing sign language accompaniment for a speech so hearing-impaired members of the audience might follow along.

'But you know, my sign language knowledge is rusty. It's been so many years since I learned it in school. Even then I wasn't best at it,' Banta demurred.

'Arre yaar, just improvise if you don't know something. They won't know the difference,' the friend reassured him, adding, 'you know, the guy who is coming to speak this evening is deadly boring. Last time when I was doing the signs for his speech, half the audience had fallen asleep by the time he was 10 minutes in. I had a hard time keeping awake myself, in fact, that is the only precaution you have to take—don't fall asleep!'

Banta was somehow induced to stand in for his friend. The evening began. It was an elite gathering for a social fundraiser. The cream of the city's society was in attendance. The evening's speaker was first introduced via a couple of speeches, which Banta managed to sign with what he thought was surprising success. Then the featured speaker took to the podium.

As he began to speak, the entire audience had turned

towards Banta, regarding his actions first with growing puzzlement, then with outright unease. His gestures and accompanying facial expressions seemed, to put it delicately, completely out of place in polite company. Some of the ladies were fainting. The speaker was still gazing over at the audience, aghast at this response, wondering what it was he could have said to outrage them so much, when he had barely begun speaking. Some of the organizers took charge, hustling Banta Singh off the stage, while others fanned out to pacify the audience.

In the wings, a visibly irate senior organizer was shaking Banta Singh by the shoulders, 'What the hell do you think you were doing out there?'

'But…I was only imitating what the gentleman spoke,' Banta protested.

'I didn't hear him say anything obscene…and he had barely started his speech anyway. What did he say?'

'Oye sirjee, he said, "It gives me great pleasure,"' Banta said, shrugging his shoulders. 'I had forgotten what the sign language was, so I improvised.'

Commentary

It is popular to decry dichotomies, but sometimes it looks like they are the very basis of our civilization. A fair part of good breeding consists of building up the strength to refrain from acting out our urges. As someone wrote, politeness comprises the ability to hide our contempt for others. Such suppression, which psychologists call repression, can lead to strange outbursts. It is no surprise that the more 'advanced' a society, the brisker the psychiatric trade. As the joke goes, 'Neurotics build castles in the air; psychotics live in them; and psychiatrists collect the rent.' In some societies, specific days of the year are set up to work out the madness (the dichotomy) from one's system, openly and without shame. The carnivals in Latin countries, Holi in India, the Mardi Gras in New Orleans and South America, all seem to point in this direction.

'In India, we don't have sex, we have 700 million people,' a young Indian American college-mate remarked many years ago, capturing an entire national paradox in one tiny sentence.

Which is all very well. But as with all things Indian, there is a parallel world alongside; where rape and misconduct with women is commonplace. An argument can reasonably be made that the din of sexual references, imagery and innuendos is not without its influence. As this is being written, news comes of two girls being gangraped and killed by hanging from a tree, in the Indian state of Uttar Pradesh. In his defence, Banta Singh was quite innocently responding to the exigencies of a difficult translation. There are giant businesses specifically engaged in making profits from dispensing exactly the fare he provided inadvertently.

As G.K. Chesterton noted: 'A sophistry may affect the mind, but an obscenity must affect the mind; it is a violence. It may do one of two things equally direct and instinctive; it may shock purity or it may inflame impurity.

But in both cases the process is brutal and irrational... The human victim is drugged—or he is sick.'[47]

What's Aap[48] with the New Nomenclature?

Banta Singh returns home late one evening. He has with him a friend from out of town, whom he has brought along insisting that he stay the night at his place.

They reach the apartment, and Banta rings the doorbell. There is no answer. He tries ringing a few times more, without success. He shakes his head, then knocks loudly on the door, shouting, '*Oye, main kiha Google Kaureh, jara darwaja tah khol de* (Hey Mrs Google, at least open the door)!'

No answer. He tries again, 'Oye Googal Kaureh!' There is still no answer, but the friend is curious. Google Kaur? He asks Banta about it.

'*Aho. Aa tah meri biwi nu main naan ditti hai.* ^&%$^ *jaddon ik swaal puchhaan te hajaar jawaab deh dindi hai* (Oh, yes. This is just my wife I've named so. Ask her one ^&%$^ question and she gives thousands of answers).'

---

[47]'Automatic Evil' by G.K. Chesterton, *Daily News*, 19 February 1910
[48]'Aap' meaning 'thou'

The friend is confused about how he should respond. Meanwhile, Banta is trying other means to get his wife's attention.

'*Oye, Facebookkaa di ma* (Hey, Mother of Facebook)!' he hollers as he bangs his fist against the door.

Still no answer. But the friend is certainly intrigued. Banta turns and notices his puzzlement.

'*Ohoi, puttar sadda* (Just my son),' he explains. '*Ik gal je ohnnu dassaan punj min't'ch saare muhalle vich phail jaandi hai* (I tell him something and five minutes later it's all over the neighbourhood).'

Meanwhile there is no progress in getting the door answered. Banta reluctantly decides to play his final card.

'Oye, beta Twitteruhhh...', he trills. 'Oye, puttar Twitteruhhhh...'

The friend tries to imagine what this could be. Banta looks at him. '*Oye, t'eeh saaddi* (My daughter)... *Lagda e'laake'ch saare munde ohde pichhe lagge hoye ne* (Looks like every boy in the area is following her).'

Commentary

The joke does a fine job of capturing the duality in all things; there is nothing which can be called an unalloyed blessing. Even spouses and children come with the potential for irritation. Particularly, things that we depend upon and rely on most are the ones most apt to cause us the greatest vexation. Oliver Goldsmith said it best:

Each to the favourite happiness attends,

And spurns the plan that aims at other ends;
Till, carried to excess in each domain,
This favourite good begets peculiar pain.

It is a truism that we are in a world of email and social media from which no one is exempt. The consequences of such an existence have hardly been thought through; meanwhile millions and millions of people throng to their attractions. What this portends for individual privacy, interactions, indeed even relationships, is fearsome to contemplate.

Downsisingh

One bright, sunny, Friday evening, a sardar walked into a bar in London.

Settling down on a bar stool, he ordered three glasses of beer. The bartender, assuming he was going to carry them back to his table, placed the order in front of him. To his surprise, he found the sardar continuing to sit right there, sipping each of the glasses in turn.

When he was done emptying all three glasses, he signalled to the bartender for a refill. The bartender, a kindly soul, had a spot of advice for the new customer. 'Y'know mate, beer tends to go flat. You'd be better off ordering one at a time, f'y'don't mind me saying so.'

The sardar was not in the least bit offended. He smiled at the bartender. 'You see, my friend, it's like this. I have two brothers. One is now in Dubai and the other in Sydney. When we parted ways, we decided that all three of us will keep our tradition, of the days when we would get together every Friday evening and down a few beers together. So, while I do this here, my two brothers are doing the same thing in Dubai and Sydney.'

The bartender seemed chastened by the sardar's response. He placed three beers in front of the sardar right away with a wide smile, saying, 'Y'know mate, twenty years I've worked in this bar and this is the best story I've ever heard. Enjoy, and let me know anything you need, d'ye hear?' The sardar smiled back, raised the first glass and took a sip, proceeding to do so with the other two glasses in sequence.

And so began a weekly ritual which in time became a famous institution of the establishment. Every Friday the sardar would come in, sit at the bar and order three beers at a time and go through multiple rounds, raising each glass at the beginning of each round.

Then one Friday evening some years later, the sardar came in as usual and settled into his customary perch. As the bartender leaned across saying cheerfully, 'Three beers coming right up, mate,' the sardar shook his head and put up his hand with two fingers raised, saying, 'just two beers, please,' with a solemn face.

The bartender blanched as he realized the implications of what he had just heard. His face became, at once, serious and tender. 'Hey mate, it must be tough…I am so, so, sorry about your loss,' he said softly.

It was the sardar's turn to be taken aback. He thought for a moment and then threw his head back, laughing. 'Oh, no, no, no, no, no. It's nothing like that. Both my brothers are fine. It is just that…I have decided to stop drinking!'

(This joke is reputed to have won first-place in a joke competition in London.)

Commentary

You can quibble over this joke being awarded the first prize instead of your favourite, but there is no denying its extraordinary import. It distills into a laugh, the most profound elements of spiritual and psychological discourse.

The idea that the act of carrying out a task is informed by the spirit in which it is undertaken, was highlighted most famously by the Bhagavad-Gita:

Karmanye vadhikaraste, Ma phaleshu kadachana,
Ma karma phala hetur bhur, Ma tey sangostva akarmani.

(Translation)
You have the right to your acts, not to the fruits thereof,
Let not for the fruits your actions be, nor be attached to inaction thou.

Here the sardar is attempting the most difficult of tests, detachment. He is drinking on behalf of his two brothers, but not for himself. It is a phenomenal concept. It is also at the foundation of Gandhi's idea of trusteeship.

'Supposing, I have come by a fair amount of wealth—either by way of legacy, or by means of trade and industry—I must know that all that wealth does not belong to me; what belongs to me is the right to an honourable livelihood, no better than that enjoyed by millions of others. The rest of my wealth belongs to the community and must be used for the welfare of the community.

'The question, how many can be real trustees according to this definition, is beside the point. If the theory is true, it is immaterial whether many live up to it or only one man lives up to it. The question is of conviction. There is nothing in this theory which can be said to be beyond the grasp of intellect, though you may say it is difficult of practice.'[49]

If we are to understand, the sardar was hitherto drinking two drinks out of each round in a spirit of detachment, and enjoying for his own purpose only his own. If indeed he had managed to do so, he deserves to be called a giani[50].

Indian philosophy is full of fables where an ostensibly pleasurable activity is pursued, but entirely in the spirit of sacrifice and not voluptuousness. Take this story of Adi Sankara's encounter with the logician Mandana Mishra in the eighth century AD. After a spirited debate lasting several days between two intellects evenly matched, Mishra was forced to concede defeat eventually. However, Mishra's wife, Ubhaya Bharati, a highly educated and erudite lady whom both contestants had accepted as judge, demurred. She declared that an ascetic like Sankara, whose monastic rules enjoined celibacy, could hardly be considered an overall master as he would lack knowledge of the art and science of love and sex. Upon this, Sankara is reputed to have set out to gain the said experience before resuming the contest. Entering the body of a dead king, he lived out a married life for sufficient time to acquire familiarity with this area of knowledge, before returning to the debate with Mishra, whom he then defeated comprehensively. Obviously, Sankara did not go back to the marital life once he had vanquished his opponent. To him it was a dispassionate excursion into passion, so to speak, solely

---

[49]Harijan, 3 June 1939
[50]Wise/learned person

for a larger purpose.

Closer to our own times, the likes of Secret Agent 007 are shown in the movies making merry with the choicest embodiments of female flesh; all in the cause, their employers would hope and have us believe, of the national interest!

Trusteeship may just as soon demand undertaking unpleasant roles, with equal disdain for one's own interest. There is a nice line from Ghalib which captures this latter situation:

Hua raqeeb toh ho, naamabar hai kya, kahiye?

(Translation)
Say, if someone becomes a rival, can he be a messenger?

Looks like he can! It fell to Vice President Al Gore in January 2001 to declare his rival George W. Bush the winner of the American presidential race after the formal electoral college count. It had been a bitter election followed by an even more contentious battle over the Florida imbroglio. In the end, after deciding not to fight further following the US Supreme Court judgment, flawed as it seemed to many, Gore, in his capacity as president of the US. Senate, presided over the counting of the electoral college votes, and pronounced Bush the winner.

The individual had given way to the trustee.

Acknowledgments

This book was kick-started by an e-mail from Kapish Mehra of Rupa Publications, urging a follow-up to *Bantaism*.

Sneha Gusain has been a patient and painstaking editor, unfailingly courteous. It was equally pleasant to work with Ritu Vajpeyi-Mohan and Amrita Mukerji.

My nephew, all of twenty years old, gave me wise lessons in drafting.

My wife and children remain doughty companions in a tough journey. My sister and nephew have cheerfully, and repeatedly, sacrificed their own comfort and convenience for my sake. Amma and Perima have borne up under immense challenges, giving me strength in turn. And it is impossible to overstate the extent of encouragement and cheer brought about by extended family and extraordinary friends.

The devotion and care of Chaudhary, Mukesh and Jagdish, the delicious food served up daily by Shekhar, my physical therapist Nasir's knowledge and skill, the solicitude of other kind souls such as Ratna, Hira Lal, Puran and Prakash, are among memories of this time which will stay with me.

www.ingramcontent.com/pod-product-compliance
Lightning Source LLC
Chambersburg PA
CBHW050558170426
43201CB00011B/1735